D1452147

DOCKS AND PORTS:2
LONDON

A typical 'flat-iron' motor collier owned by the CEGB, the *Harry Richardson*, 1,777grt, built in 1930, passes under Westminster Bridge in 1965. *CEGB*

DOCKS AND PORTS:2
LONDON

W. Paul Clegg

LONDON

IAN ALLAN LTD

Left:
**A view of London and St Katharine Docks (top)
looking west, in the early 1950s. Although the latter
is virtually empty, there is plenty of traffic in
London Dock.** *PLA Collection, Museum of London*

Contents

First published 1987

ISBN 0 7110 1673 9

Published by Ian Allan Ltd, Shepperton, Surrey; and printed by Ian Allan Printing Ltd at their works at Coombelands in Runnymede, England

Front cover, top:
Baco-Liner 2 seen at Tilbury on her first visit at Easter 1986. *Port of London Authority*

Front cover, bottom:
A view of the Royal Group of Docks c1950. *PLA Collection, Museum of London*

Right:
The 35,677 gross ton Cunard liner Mauretania entering King George V Docks, after her first trans-Atlantic crossing — the largest ship to berth here — on 6 August 1939. It was to be her only visit. Three unidentified 'Sun' tugs (W. H. J. Alexander) are in attendance at the stern. *PLA Collection, Museum of London*

Acknowledgements

I am most grateful to the host of people who have assisted, knowingly and willingly, in one way or another, with the provision of information and illustrations for this book.

The well-used phrase 'without whose help publication would not have been possible' was never more true, and is sincerely meant. I would particularly like to thank the following, and apologise for any inadvertent omissions (names are not listed in any order of priority):

Bob Aspinall, Chris Blamey and Terry Hatton (Port of London Authority); Irene Shaw (Museum of London); Vicky Furey (London Docklands Development Corporation).

Barry Jaynes (The London Wharfingers' Association); Peter Home (Purfleet Deep Wharf); Robert Kimber (Scruttons and Victoria Deep Wharf); Ron Pratt (Ford Motor Company), D. F. Firmin (Phoenix Wharf); Mike Taylo: (Convoys); Alan Hawkins (Denton Wharf).

Stephen Rabson (P&O); Alfred Flint (Blundel and Crompton); Rowland Brown (Cunard Archivist, University of Liverpool); Tony Walker (Finanglia Ferries); Bill Ennis (C. R. Ennis).

Gratitude goes also to my wife and famil for not only their moral support but als practical assistance, and finally to a respecte and long-suffering publisher, with whom i has always been a pleasure to work.

W. Paul Clegg
Ashburton 198

Introduction

The history of the Port of London has been written many times since the mid-1850s and, for the most part, publications have followed much the same pattern. The publisher and author of this publication hope that readers will find it different in a number of respects. First, it is basically pictorial in nature, although at the same time the text is designed to be sufficiently comprehensive as to enable the reader to follow easily the background to what has taken place. Not too much stress has been placed on the legal aspects of the growth of the port, except where they affect the building of docks or the enforcement of navigational procedures. On the other hand, few histories so far have dealt specifically with a number of ancillary activities, such as shipbuilding, pleasure craft and port users. Although a number of these topics is covered here, it is not possible to incorporate everything in a book of this size: if a reader's particular interest is only glossed over, please accept our apologies.

This is the first book known to be published after the closure of the entire PLA upper docks system. Given that Tilbury will continue to operate in the foreseeable future, the story in this respect is complete.

The story of the port as a whole can be divided into a number of periods of history, depending on one's outlook. The author has chosen to present it basically in five parts, as indicated in the List of Contents. It should be remembered that London as a whole has always handled more cargo than any other port in the United Kingdom, with one totally misleading exception. In the ports' league table for 1984, it was shown that Sullom Voe, in the Shetland Islands, actually handled more tonnage than anywhere else, totalling 59,682 million tonnes — but of this, only about 11,000 tonnes consisted of cargoes other than oils! Second in the same league table came London, with a total tonnage (excluding oils) of 18.46 million tonnes; Tees and Hartlepool came

third (11.02 million tonnes); while fourth was Grimsby and Immingham (9.79 million tonnes). Felixstowe was fifth with 7.48 million tonnes. The total trade of London in 1984, including oils, was over 43 million tonnes, and it was claimed at a 'Use of the River Thames' conference held in London in 1985 that more cargo passed through the Thames Barrier upstream alone than passed over the quays at Felixstowe!

In spite of the reduction in PLA facilities to incorporate Tilbury only, it is a fact that the Port of London Authority *per se* is handling more conventional and container cargoes than all the private wharves put together, though it cannot be denied that the gap is closing.

It has to be remembered that the PLA is responsible not only for providing facilities at Tilbury for cargo handling, but is also the body which has the task of providing navigational facilities (through the Thames Navigation Service), of dredging channels, of licensing wharfingers, of salvage and of keeping the river clear of driftwood, to name but a few. Hence, as port users will know, conservancy dues on ships using the port are charged by the PLA, regardless of whether they are going into Tilbury or to a private wharf. The PLA is responsible for these activities for a distance seawards of some 150km (94 miles) from Teddington.

One point may need clarification. The term 'Port of London' is often confused with 'Port of London Authority'. The two are different. The former encompasses the entire port area including oil refineries, private wharves, riverside storage and factories, and the Port of London Authority premises. The latter therefore is self-evident.

This book is based not only on historical records but also on the author's experience of many years' work as a shipping agent in London. Hopefully, the result will find acceptance among readers.

Origins–to 1800

Although small open boats will have been used on the River Thames for many thousands of years, it is probable that the Romans founded the port of London as we know it today. Following the partial success of their second invasion in 54BC (the first, a year earlier, achieved little), the Roman armies under Julius Caesar moved north and west from their landing point on the Kent coast, until they reached the Thames. Moving further west, they crossed the river at the first convenient crossing point, close to where London Bridge is now. This established a point for the first bridge which was to be built later.

Following Caesar's withdrawal because of problems in Gaul and at home, there was a breathing space until the turn of the century, after which the Emperor Claudius invaded yet again and incorporated Britain officially in the Roman Empire in AD43. It is believed that a wooden bridge across the Thames was built shortly afterwards, which had a drawbridge in the middle for tall ships. Buildings including housing and commercial premises began to

spring up on the high ground around the north end of the bridge. The land on the south side — mostly marsh — was not to be developed for a long time to any great extent. London was named Londinium, and the river received its own name — Tamesis.

By Hadrian's time (AD121), London had grown to some considerable size, and later was encircled by a defensive stone wall. Also, and most important, trade began to develop and ships from other continental ports and even further afield brought supplies and goods, for both the occupying army and the civilian population, in ever increasing amounts. While smaller ships would have sat on mud flats on the north bank both above and below the bridge, larger ships would float at anchor and discharge to small barges or 'lighters' thus laying the foundations for a system which was

Below:
The City and Port of London as it is believed to have looked in Hadrian's time, about 120 AD. The 'quays' below London Bridge were to survive, in altered form, for nearly 2,000 years. *Museum of London*

to last virtually to the present day. As the size of ships grew, more port activity developed downstream of the bridge, and it is believed that quays were built along what became the Billingsgate stretch of the riverbank. There were no embankments along the river until much later. The mouth of the River Fleet was used as a cargo handling area.

And so the port grew in importance, as did London, until the Romans left in about AD410, by which time the city covered some 340 acres and sheltered an estimated population of over 5,000 within its walls.

Even before the Romans' withdrawal, Saxon invaders had proved troublesome, using the Thames as a means of reaching London. Afterwards, during the 'Dark Ages', London declined in importance and was open to invasion by all comers. First came the Saxons, who, by early in the 7th century, had re-established some sort of civilised living involving commerce and trade, and London revived in Anglo-Saxon times despite constant disruption caused by Danish Viking raids. It was during this period that tolls are known to have been imposed on ships using the quays, and on goods. The tolls, payable to the Crown, consisted of both cash payments and kind, usually taken from the cargo the ship was carrying. Wool became a prime export, alongside skins and cereals, while imports consisted of a variety of goods, including wine, cloth, timber, fish and finished goods including clothing.

Although the Danes held London for a short time, from 1016 when Canute became king, the Saxons regained control in 1042. But not for long. Only 22 years later the last Saxon king, Harold II, lost Britain to William of Normandy at the Battle of Hastings, and it was under his astute administration that London again began to prosper. Defence was a priority, so substantial castles were built at each end of the Roman wall on the north bank of the Thames: Baynard's Castle in the west and the White Tower of the Tower of London in the east, completed in around 1078. It is said that these castles were built as much for defence against the King's subjects as against foreign invaders. As the population grew, so did shipping on the river, and the range of goods being handled over the quays broadened to include luxuries such as silks, spices and ivory from the Middle East and, eventually, the Far East.

Henry II was on the throne when the first stone bridge was built — the well documented London Bridge with shops, houses and a chapel on deck. Completed in 1209 (30 years passed between inception and completion) it was fitted with a drawbridge to allow ships to pass through, but this fell into disuse and was later removed.

Another feature of the bridge which affected shipping was the large number of supporting piers which prevented the river flowing at its former pace: the water, when on the ebb, tended to pile up on the upstream side of the

bridge as it forced its way through the arches. This created turbulent conditions on the east side of the bridge, and the force of the water helped to dredge the bottom thereby creating a greater depth of water leading to easier access for deeper draughted ships and the creation of the 'Pool' of London. Curiously, it seems that the effect in the reverse direction, on the flood tide, was less significant, due no doubt to the fact that the tide was fighting the flow of the river.

Over the years, further quays were developed along the north side, between the two castles, and small docks or inlets were cut into the bank to increase berthing space, that at Billingsgate (constructed later) being the largest. However, congestion was becoming an increasing problem, and it became the practice for most ships — becoming bigger as time passed — to moor in the river and land cargo by small boat. As the port grew, so did ancillary activities, such as warehousing, packing and insurance. In addition, trading became well established, so that the city became a centre of commerce for foreign merchants, many of whom, from Italy, France, Germany and other places, settled and made it their home. There also appeared at this time the first Customs House, built in 1382 at Wool Wharf near what is now Sugar Quay. Coal began to arrive in increasing quantities by small sailing ships from the northeast, thus laying the foundations of what was to become a most significant feature of cargo handling in

the Port of London in later centuries. The City of London and its Guilds began to take certain rights and privileges (including control of the port) away from the Crown, so that there was a shift of power.

But still more ships were crowding into the 'Pool' of London and berthing space became increasingly difficult to secure. The problem was made worse by the ferry boats, which carried passengers not only short distances, but also as far as Greenwich and Gravesend.

When the Tudor period dawned, there developed an age of expansion and excitement. Trade with the continent increased — as it did with countries further afield — and the population of London was about 50,000 when Henry VIII came to the throne in 1509. A hundred years later this had grown to nearly 200,000, of whom 40,000 are estimated to have earned their living by being connected with the port and river one way or another. Henry VIII caused Royal dockyards to be constructed at Woolwich and Deptford in 1512 and 1515 respectively, and it was at the latter that Elizabeth I knighted Francis Drake on board his ship *Golden Hind* after his circumnavigation of the world during 1572-80. Perhaps the most significant events to take place during this period were the granting of Arms to the Company of Watermen in 1585, and the signing of the Royal Charter for the East India Co at the end of 1599. Both these acts were undertaken by Elizabeth I, for it was during her reign that much overseas activity

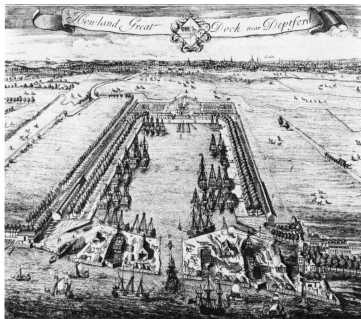

Left:
Deptford Dockyard seen much as it must have looked in Henry VIII's time.
Museum of London

Right:
The Howland Great Dock, near Deptford, in about 1720. The absence of any kind of handling equipment and warehousing indicates that no cargo was loaded or discharged here.
Museum of London

originated, though it was Henry VIII who had founded the Royal Navy as an establishment separate from the merchant navy in about 1515. The Watermen were skilled in handling barges without sail, but solely with oars through the congested waters, and often against tides, dealing with treacherous currents the meanwhile.

Another important feature of this period was the designation of the so-called 'Legal Quays', by an Act of Parliament dated 1558, the year before Queen Mary was replaced by Elizabeth I. A total of 1,464ft of quayage below London Bridge, on the north bank of the river as far as the Tower, was selected for this purpose, over which all cargo (excepting fish) had to pass. Customs officers were appointed to oversee the loading and unloading of ships. The reason for this arrangement was that the chaos and congestion on the river had led to smuggling on a grand scale, and revenue was being lost. Later, Billingsgate became famous for the handling only of fish. By the 1790s, the entire riverbank constituted Legal Quays from London Bridge to include what is now Sugar Quay, the Custom House by now having been moved to its present site. The river frontage of the Tower itself was never part of these Legal Quays.

As the East India Co developed, its ships became larger, and usually they were unable to travel further upstream than Blackwall, so that cargo was barged up to the Legal Quays. The company enjoyed a monopoly of trade with India and beyond, and was later granted permission to arm its ships. It was later to have its own river moorings, offices and wharf with a private shipbuilding yard at Blackwall, established in 1612, which was to build a large number of East India Co ships. This was the same year in which the Shipwright's Company was established on the Thames.

In the meantime, congestion also led to the establishment of a number of wharves on the south (right) bank of the river, in areas of Southwark and Rotherhithe, which had hitherto been principally marshland. These were regarded as 'sufferance quays' by Customs, so that should any untoward or illegal activities be discovered, permission could be withdrawn. Interestingly, much the same situation obtains today, where a riverside wharf may traditionally have Customs authority to land timber and/or paper products, but if it is required to land, say, packaged steel plates, special dispensation must be sought from HM Customs in advance, in writing. This will usually be granted, but it cannot be assumed.

Although, in hindsight, it would seem

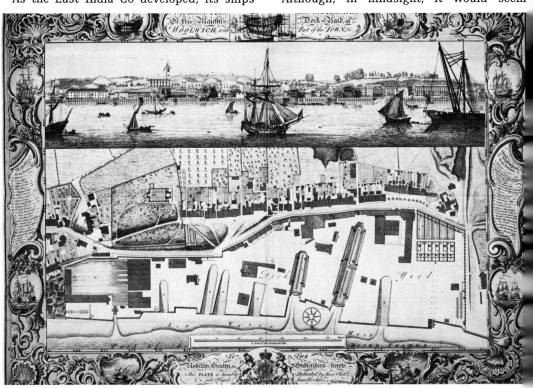

obvious that, to relieve congestion in the Pool, wet docks equipped for handling cargo should have been constructed, it is curious that although two such docks were constructed by the turn of the 17th century, neither was so fitted out. The first of these to be opened was that operated by the East India Co at Blackwall, alongside the shipbuilding yard, in about 1680. The second was a private venture on the south bank at Rotherhithe, known as the Howland Great Wet Dock, subsequently to become part of the Greenland Dock in the later Surrey Commercial Docks system. This was

Above:
Trinity House, founded by Henry VIII in 1514, moved offices several times until moving into the present office on Tower Hill, built in 1795. *Author*

opened in about 1698. According to contemporary prints, both docks were tree-lined (to protect shipping from the high winds) and there is no sign of sheds, warehousing or any other kind of cargo-handling activity. In fact, the purpose of these docks was basically to repair ships, careen when necessary and fit out ships built elsewhere. Thus, in no way was commercial congestion relieved.

Between 1700 and 1800 the number of ships arriving to load or discharge cargoes (London has always been an importer rather than an exporter) rose from 1,350 to 3,650, and still there were no additional facilities: ships just had to moor in the river, and still had to land cargoes over the Legal Quays. Clearly, something had to be done, not only because of the congestion, but also because critics of Legal Quay operators claimed that they were in a position to charge exorbitant dues because of the monopolistic situation. Similarly, congestion was experienced on the quays where cargoes often sat for lengthy periods, without cover, before being examined by Customs

and/or being collected by importers or their agents.

Everyone was becoming increasingly concerned with pilferage (which enforcement of the Legal Quay system did not entirely eliminate), and lengthy delays in the landing and shore-handling of cargoes. Merchants involved in the West India trade were particularly critical, since their principal cargo — sugar — tended to arrive in large convoys during the season of prevailing winds, from July to October. War with France was another difficulty which had to be faced — hence the 'convoy' system. Thus it was hardly surprising that those whose interests lay in trades with the West Indies were among the first to press for better facilities. In 1793 a committee was drawn up with the express purpose of persuading Parliament to act, with the net result that in 1799 an Act of Parliament created the West India Dock Co, which immediately set about the creation of the West India Docks.

As will be seen, others followed in quick succession. Further docks were constructed and — at long last — after centuries of congestion and delays — sufficient facilities were provided for the expeditious handling of ships and cargoes.

Thames Passenger
Services

Above:
Dissatisfaction with river services at the turn of the century caused the LCC to set up its own organisation and it ordered 30 paddle steamers, similar to the *Purcell* here. Services started in 1905, but were not successful, and were withdrawn by the end of 1907. *Author's Collection*

Below:
General Steam's (Eagle Steamers) ps *Royal Eagle*, built in 1932, regularly served between Tower Pier, Southend, Margate, Ramsgate and Felixstowe, and could carry up to 1,987 passengers at a speed of 19kt. She survived the war and was eventually withdrawn in 1950. *Author's Collection*

Right:

The small *Crested Eagle*, built in 1938, was in the Eagle Steamers' fleet from 1948 to 1957. In earlier postwar years she was particularly associated with the PLA docks cruises around the Royals from Tower Pier, which the latter had started in 1930.
Author's Collection

m.v. CRESTED EAGLE

Below:

Eagle Steamers' *Royal Daffodil*, dating from 1939, started her working career on day excursions to Ostend. She was one of three remaining at the end of 1966 when Eagle Steamers ceased operations. The others were *Queen of the Channel*, built in 1948, and *Royal Sovereign*, built in 1949. The *Daffodil* is seen here moored in the Thames awaiting the start of the 1962 season. *Author*

Right:

London Hoverservices operated HM2 sidewall hovercraft on services from Tower Pier between July 1973 and October 1974. Each craft could carry up to 65 passengers at 30kt and one of them is seen here off Greenwich Pier in August 1974. *Author*

Above:
Berthed at St Katharine's Pier is the Russian-built hydrofoil *Raketa of Greenwich* in August 1974. After a trial period during 1974, Speed Hydrofoils took over the runs formerly served by London Hoverservices in October, but this was also unsuccessful too, and services closed in September **1976.** *Author*

Below:
After Eagle Steamers' withdrawal at the end of the 1966 season, there had been little chance for passengers to travel all the way down river. However, the privately owned ps *Waverley*, built in 1947, has been making welcome appearances for a few weeks in either spring or autumn since 1978. *Author*

II

The First Enclosed Docks Era 1799-1850

As has been seen in the previous chapter, merchants were becoming increasingly concerned at the lack of space in the Port of London. Given that London, as a city and a port, was fast becoming a world leader in commerce, those concerned were complaining that other UK ports — notably Bristol and Liverpool — were offering better facilities. Even worse, in the past, fears were expressed that continental ports, particularly Antwerp, would begin to accept cargoes for London on a trans-shipment basis, whereby London car-goes would be sent over to the capital in small ships, the cargo having been off-loaded there by deep-sea ships.

A number of schemes for enclosed docks were proposed, but in the event the West India Dock Co was first from the starting line, in spite of protests from owners of the Legal Quays. The Company of Watermen, *inter alia*, was also against the enclosed docks scheme. The City Corporation, and various guilds, similarly opposed any plan which might limit the force of their monopoly of certain aspects

Right:
East India Dock, showing the mast house, as it looked before conversion to a commercial cargo-handling dock. All workers appear to be employed in ship-repair work.
Museum of London

Below:
West India Dock in about 1805, probably viewed from the western (Limehouse) entrance. Note the prominent warehouses.
Museum of London.

of the shipping business. Thus it took time before anything of substantial interest was finally accepted.

The West India Dock Act of 1799 authorised two parallel docks across the Isle of Dogs; in addition, there was to be a canal to the south of, and parallel to, the authorised docks, so that ships bound for the upper reaches of the Thames (ie the Pool) would be saved the time taken by the long haul around the southern tip of the Isle of Dogs. The canal was financed by the Corporation of the City of London, while the two docks were to be promoted and completed entirely by private enterprise. At this time, before the old London Bridge was abolished, and long before Tower Bridge was erected, there was still a great deal of argument against the proposals for building cargo handling docks, bearing in mind that the only two wet-docks built so far on the Thames (Great Howland and East India) were for shipbuilding and repairing work only. The London Dock Act of 1800 authorised a dock at Wapping, thus competing directly with the West India Dock Co's proposals, so that even at this early stage competition became more blatant.

Of course, vested interests in the old way of doing things fought hard, but to no avail. The Isle of Dogs is not, in fact, an island, though the building of West India Dock virtually made it so. The name Millwall, as it applies particularly to the southwestern corner of the peninsula, relates specifically to the fact that a number of windmills were located there to drain the land and to provide grain-crushing facilities. William Jessop (1745-1814) was appointed engineer for the West India Docks and an equally well known John Rennie (1761-1821) acted as consultant. William Pitt the Younger, then Prime Minister, laid the foundation stone in July 1800 — followed by the usual gargantuan reception. The official opening of the West India (Import) Dock took place in June 1802, when the first West Indiaman arrived with a cargo of sugar. It was at about this time that it was agreed that duties should be paid on goods such as wine

Left:
Built in 1808, the building at the main entrance to the West India Dock was designed for the use of Customs but has since been in use as the Dock Manager's offices. *Author*

Below:
An aquatint of London Dock dating from 1808, looking east. Note the warehouses and high surrounding walls to prevent theft. This is the later Western Dock, with the original entrance through Wapping Basin on the right.
Museum of London

only when they were withdrawn from the warehouses for consumption, not when they were landed. The Warehousing Act of 1803 designated the buildings at West India Dock as 'licensed bonded warehouses'. In the meantime, the West India Dock Co had succeeded in breaking the monopoly of the Legal Quays, the 1799 Act having provided that all West India trade, both import and export, should be handled within the dock area. The second (Export) dock — now known as 'Middle Section' — was completed in 1806. Furthermore, trade continued to grow, petty theft had been reduced to the lowest levels yet, and a dock company police force was established. But there was another improvement, as ships were being discharged within days rather than weeks. London City Corporation became interested in this venture, which was then 'out of town', and agreed to the cutting of the City Canal across the Isle of Dogs to the south of the existing Export Dock. It was not a success, saved little time and was not worth the investment of nearly £170,000, but the City was not to know that at the time. No dues were payable during the first few years so the canal was reasonably well used. After the imposition of dues the tonnage fell rapidly so that in 1829 the City Corporation sold the canal to the West India Dock Co, which eventually enlarged it and incorporated it into the West India Dock system as the South West India Dock (later known as the 'Main Section') in 1870. The eastern lock entrance to the canal eventually became the only entrance to the entire West India and Millwall system.

There was provision for entering and leaving the two original docks both from the west via Limehouse Basin, and from the east via Blackwall Basin. From each basin there was a separate entrance into each dock, there being no connecting channel between the two docks until much later. In practice, the eastern entrance was used by ships to or from sea, while the Limehouse Basin lock was for the use of lighters proceeding up-river, having taken on their cargoes from alongside ships in the dock. It was a very good arrangement. The docks were built on a grand scale, as were other major works throughout the land in this era of expansion. They had a length of almost half-a-mile, a width of 500ft (Import Dock) and 400ft (Export Dock), and could take ships with a draught of up to 29ft. The Import Dock in particular was well provided for, with several five-storey warehouses on the North Quay alone, having a total length of about 930yd — nearly the full length of the dock. High walls deterred thieves.

There were two features of particular importance in the long term in the West India Dock Act, and in other Acts which were to follow. The first of these, and arguably the most significant, was that which allowed free access to and from the docks for lighters and barges which were carrying cargoes, and was known as the 'Free Water Clause'. It was clearly designed to permit lightermen the same freedom of movement which they enjoyed on the river. As long as the dock companies retained their monopoly of their own particular cargoes (eg ships to and from the West Indies had to be handled by the West India Dock Co) — the second important feature of the early Docks Acts — the fact that lighters had free movement and the dock companies were earning no revenue therefrom mattered little. But when monopolies began to be taken away the docks did begin to suffer. Although strenuous efforts were made to have the 'Free Water Clause' removed, they were never successful; although import and export cargo lighterage on the Thames has virtually died out, the clause still applies to this day.

———

As the West India Dock Co was forging ahead with its plans and dock construction, other schemes saw the light of day, and the London Dock and Surrey Docks followed in quick succession. Also, by now, further Legal Quays on the Thames had been granted a licence, including a number on the South Bank.

Although the building of the proposed London Dock presented no technical problems, there was another difficulty: the intended area for use at Wapping was fully built up, and home for people and businesses. Their removal was costly and time consuming. The London Dock Act received Royal Assent in 1800, and the foundation stone was laid in June 1802 by Henry Addington, then Prime Minister, who in the same month also opened the West India Dock. The London Dock was open for traffic in January 1805, with the usual 21-year monopoly, this time relating to brandy, rice, tobacco and wine which did not come from either the East or the West Indies. Again, extensive warehousing featured in the plans (notable for their wine vaults), together with an extremely high protective wall, much of which still survives today. Although Daniel Alexander (1768-1846), London-born, was appointed surveyor, John Rennie was involved on a consultancy basis. The layout of the dock itself was complex, there being a Western Dock separated from a smaller Eastern Dock by a

Above:
The 'Round House' in West India Dock is believed to have served either as a lock-up for thieves or a store for gunpowder. There were originally two which dated from about 1810. *Author*

small dock designated for the exclusive use of the tobacco trade — hence Tobacco Dock. The Western Dock was linked with the Thames by locks through Wapping Basin, closed later, while there was a second set of locks joining the Western Dock with the river via the Hermitage Basin at the southwest corner of the dock. Access to the Eastern Dock was by yet a third set of locks through the Eastern Basin. Both Eastern and Hermitage entrances remained in use until the dock closed. In 1831 the capacity of Western Dock was increased by the building of a central pier abutting on to the west quay.

———

It will be remembered from the previous chapter that the East India Co had established itself at Blackwall, where the dock was for shiprepairing and laying-up purposes only and was not used for cargo-handling. Cargo was latterly trans-shipped into lighters for landing farther up-river at the Legal Quays. However, by the 1780s, still enjoying its monopoly with Eastern trade, the company began the construction of warehouses in

London at Cutler Street, New Street (Bishopsgate) and Crutched Friars. The first two were opened in 1782, the last-named in 1789. From the time these warehouses were open, it became the practice to land cargoes at Blackwall Wharf and from there take them directly by covered carts to the appropriate warehouses. By 1790 the dock had been enlarged and renamed Brunswick Dock, but it was still used only for work on the ships themselves. No cargo was offloaded here — at least, in theory.

It is not out of place here to describe briefly the career of the East India Co which grew up during the time of the Elizabethan and subsequent explorations. With an enormous fleet of ships which developed trade, it eventually became the custodian of a large part of the British Empire. In fact, it signified the growth of the Empire, for which it was itself at least in part responsible.

Having secured its charter, together with monopoly rights, from Elizabeth I, the East India (initiated by the Lord Mayor of London and a number of merchants concerned with the East Indies trade) first carried out several excursions to the Indies, most of which brought back pepper from Amboina, an island in Indonesia. A voyage in 1608 brought the company into contact with India proper for the first time. In subsequent years there was occasional friction — sometimes developing into outright aggression — with the Portuguese explorers and traders, and with the Dutch and French East India Companies, so that in time the company withdrew from the East Indies, ousted the French from India, but at the same time established valuable trading posts in countries such as Aden, Burma, China and Singapore.

After Elizabeth, other monarchs were less enthusiastic about the company's activities, though they were happy enough to accept the revenues arising therefrom. A rival organisation had been initiated by James I as early as 1606, but this failed. In 1635 Charles I licensed yet another competitor, known as the Assada Merchants, which brought disrepute on England and the original East India Co by acts of piracy and other discreditable activities. After the Roundheads defeated Charles in the Civil War, Cromwell re-established the company's right to trade without hindrance by forming a joint-stock company, for which capital was made available in 1657.

However, this state of affairs was not to last for long. During the reign of Charles II, dissatisfaction with the company's monopolistic situation among English traders led to

19

increasing hostility towards the company, so that it became the central issue of a constitutional crisis — should the Crown or Parliament be in a position to grant charters and monopolies? Clearly, the latter's claims were clear-cut. In 1698, with the approval of William I, Parliament chartered a new rival, named The United Company, to which the old company's holdings were transferred in 1702. It is intriguing to remember that by the middle of the 18th century, India was virtually controlled outright by the new company, which administered the country, commanded the armed forces and even appointed the Governor-General. But this was not to last. The India Act of 1784 removed virtually all power in India from the company, with the notable exception of administration. Alleged mishandling of the Indian (Sepoy) Mutiny of 1857, together with the muddled handling of events leading up to it, brought the company into direct conflict with the Crown — now Queen Victoria — which assumed direct control of the Government of India the following year.

In the meantime, in the Port of London the East India Co had joined the enclosed-dock building scramble by promoting a Bill in Parliament to enable it to load and discharge cargoes in the Brunswick Dock area, a Bill which became an Act in 1803. John Rennie, again, and Ralph Walker were appointed joint engineers. The Act stipulated that cargoes should still be stored in the company's City warehouses and granted the by now usual 21-year monopoly rights for China as well as India and created a subsidiary, The East India Dock Co. By now, the company's ships had become very much bigger, nearly 800 tons, and in any case it was no longer physically possible to sail anywhere near the Pool. The provision of two docks was planned: the Brunswick Dock was to be enlarged and used for exports only, while to the north of this a new bigger dock was to be constructed for handling imports. Each was to be linked to a basin, from where a small channel, with locks, entered the Thames to the southeast of the smaller dock. The enterprise opened for business in August 1806, and it was laid down that all ships trading to and from India and China were to use these docks, and that no other ships were to be handled. The 120ft high mast-house, a relic from Brunswick Dock days and now incorporated in the Export Dock, was finally removed in 1862. Because of the requirement in the early stages that all imports should be transported to City warehouses, there was little need for the massive dockside buildings associated with the London

and West India Docks. However, after the 1820s when monopolies were removed, there was a spate of building around both parts of the East India Dock.

————

Before the East India Dock was opened, yet another scheme — this time for docks on the South Bank of the river — was proposed. It is true that there was a number of small inlets on this side of the river which had existed for some time, notably at Hays Dock, St Mary Overy and St Saviour's, but these were small and not yet developed.

The development of what became known as the Surrey Commercial Docks was piecemeal, and consequently grew as a haphazard collection of basins and harbours. At its fullest extent, the enterprise consisted of no fewer than nine docks, six timber ponds (for floating timber which had been imported, and for laying up timber lighters) and a canal nearly four miles in length. All docks in Rotherhithe were designed for, and associated with in particular, American and Russian timber trades.

The first party involved in the new docks was the Grand Surrey Canal Co, which put forward a number of grandiose schemes from 1801, including a canal linking the Thames with Portsmouth without locks! In practice, all that materialised was a canal, joined by locks with the Thames at a point roughly opposite to the eastern entrance to the London Dock, which stretched as far as Peckham, and a three-acre dock known as the Grand Surrey Basin, which was opened in 1807 at the junction of the canal with the Thames. Thus started development at the northwest rim of the Rotherhithe area, in which William Jessop among others was adviser.

Later in the same year, another separate project was advanced by the newly formed Commercial Dock Co. This involved converting the former Howland Dock for cargo handling, (Howland had been sold in about 1763 and renamed Greenland Dock for use by the whaling fleet, but this had by now left the Thames), together with the smaller Norway Dock to the north. Thus this second development was right at the southeastern corner of what was to become the final pattern — diametrically opposed to the Grand Surrey Basin. Work started on the alterations in 1808. Soon afterwards a third company, the East Country Dock Co, started building the East Country Dock, smaller than, and parallel to, Greenland Dock.

Above:
Surrey Commercial Docks in about 1830. This is Greenland Dock, viewed from near the entrance looking west. The basin leading to Norway Dock is on the far right. *Museum of London*

The fourth constituent of this chaotic situation was the Baltic Dock Owners Co, which appeared the following year, led by property owners in the northeast area. This concern built several interlinked docks and ponds, which were to have their own lock entrance to the Thames near the northeastern tip of the peninsular via Lavender. The dock area concerned included water areas better known later as Lady Dock, Acorn and Lavender Ponds, which also had large areas of storage. There followed a sequence of mergers and takeovers, as in other parts of the port, together with further development, to be referred to later. Suffice it to mention here that in 1810, the Commercial Dock Co absorbed the Baltic Dock Co.

It is worth noting at this stage that the granting of trading monopolies to dock companies ceased after the passing of the East India Dock Act of 1803, and all monopolies were cancelled outright from 1823, when the West India Dock Co's monopoly clause expired. The East India itself ceased trading later, having lost its protection, and disposed of its City warehouses to the East and West India Dock and St Katharine's Dock Co (see below).

After the removal of monopolies, a ship from any port in the world was free to berth at will, and the Legal Quays came into their own again. Having lost certain trades to the enclosed docks downriver, they were now in a position to win them back again, taking advantage of the 'Free Water Clause'. Proprie-

Below:
An engraving of about 1825 showing the proposed layout of St Katharine Dock. The reality was not very different. *Museum of London*

tors of the enclosed docks which held monopolies became anxious, and the first outward manifestation that things for them were not going too well was the amalgamation of the two India Dock Companys in 1838.

In view of the fact that there were to be no more monopolies granted, it would seem that the spate of new construction would fall off. It did not. While the companies involved in building the Surrey Docks had hoped for monopoly status, the proprietors of the final project during this period knew there was no possibility of this. Indeed quite the reverse was true; they anticipated that they would profit by the removal of monopolies. This project was for the building of St Katharine's Dock, squeezed in between London Dock and the road alongside the Tower of London (there was no Tower Bridge approach road as yet).

The St Katharine Dock Bill was passed in 1825, and the foundation stone was laid in May two years later. It was an unpopular project. It is reported that over 11,000 people had to be rehoused, and the hospital of St Katharine, originally founded in the 12th century, and which later survived the Great Fire of 1666, had to close and be pulled down. The institution moved to Regent's Park. Thomas Telford was appointed engineer for the construction works, which involved the provision of two docks (Western and Eastern), each of about four acres, linked by a basin of 1½ acres from which there was a lock entrance to the Thames. What was new about this dock was the provision of warehousing right to the edge of the quay, so that cargoes could be offloaded by overhead gallows crane from hold to appropriate floor. They were designed particularly for the handling of valuable cargoes, such as ivory, turtle shells, sugar and marble, and were surrounded by high walls to prevent theft. The road entrance to the dock system was in the northwest corner.

The dock itself was opened in October 1828 — the last enclosed dock to be completed for some considerable time.

———

In the meantime other smaller docks grew up on both sides of the river. On the south bank, within the London Bridge-Tower Bridge area, were St Mary Overy, an inlet for handling small ships from very early times which is now hardly discernible, Hay's Dock off Tooley Street, which originally had lock gates, and St Saviour's Dock below Tower Bridge. This was originally the mouth of the River Neckinger. In the 1850s all three were blessed with the provision of warehousing on a grand scale, owned by Hay's Wharf and Butler's Wharf respectively, though others filled in gaps.

On the left bank of the river, two enclosed docks outside the jurisdiction of the above-mentioned Docks Acts, were the 10-acre Limehouse Basin (or Regent's Canal Dock), halfway between London and West India Docks, and Poplar Docks on land between West India (Import) Dock and Blackwall. The former was built to accommodate barges in 1812. There cargoes were trans-shipped to canal barges for on-carriage on the Regent's Canal for the Grand Junction at Paddington, or on the Lea Navigation. The basin was subsequently enlarged several times between 1820 and 1865 to receive sea-going ships. Although it was still in use relatively recently (under the ownership of the British Waterways Board from 1963), it gradually fell into disrepair and was closed to commercial traffic by about 1970.

Below:
A scene of great activity on the Upper Pool immediately below London Bridge, in about 1840. The 'Monument' is clearly visible and steamships are already making their presence felt!
Museum of London

The Poplar Docks, which had no separate access to the Thames but was linked by a cut with the West India Dock Co's Blackwall Basin, was instituted by the railways, which had a goods depot there from the opening of the dock, mainly to handle coal, in 1852. The dock passed through successive ownerships, including the Midland and the LNER, until passing to British Railways in 1948. A second, smaller, basin was constructed to the west in 1875. This too has now fallen into disuse.

The previous pages have brought the story of the enclosed docks and riverside wharves up to 1850, as far down-river as Bow Creek. Business was not thriving, and after the completion of the St Katharines Dock no further attempts were made to promote enclosed dock schemes until 1850. The withdrawal of monopolies, and the resurgence and extension of private wharves as a result of the 'free trade' attitudes of the times, both led to financial difficulties for many parties and for the dock companies in particular. Mergers

Top:
The Regent's Canal Dock at Limehouse, in about 1825, looking north. Limehouse Church is prominent in the distance. *Museum of London*

Above:
The entrance to Regent's Canal Dock, seen from the Thames, was opened in about 1820 and finally closed in about 1969. *Author*

Left:
The entrance to the Medway Canal at Gravesend, where locks link it with the Thames. It dates from about 1824, but only pleasure craft now use the Gravesend Basin. The rest of the canal is closed. *Author*

became the order of the day. But new dock construction did not cease, due to the ever increasing size of ships and port trade generally. From the 1840s a new era of expansion developed which was to lead to the need for better facilities.

III

Consolidation, and the Second Enclosed Docks Era 1850-1908

About the turn of the half-century (1850), further new schemes arose for bigger and better docks. Some would soon be needed: the Empire was growing apace, so that trade was increasing by leaps and bounds. On the other hand, consolidation was also the order of the day — more mergers and takeovers were gradually taking place, since cut-throat competition during the third and fourth decades between docks had given rise to its own inevitable consequences. As far as navigational matters were concerned, the situation was totally chaotic, and thus the Thames Conservancy Board was born out of an Act of 1857, in an attempt to sort order out of this chaos. This body immediately set about improving piers, installing improved moorings and removing shoals. A previous Act of 1853 sanctioned 'sufference wharves' outside the docks areas and original quays, so that by 1866 a total of some 115 riverside wharves enjoyed Customs facilities. It is therefore surprising that the enclosed docks survived, but they did, due entirely to the increase in trade.

As far as mergers and takeovers were concerned, on the south bank the East Country Dock Co was absorbed by The Commercial Dock Co in 1851. Four years later, the Grand Surrey Canal was reconstituted as The Grand Surrey Docks & Canal Co which, in 1864, amalgamated with The Commercial Dock Co to form The Surrey Commercial Dock Co. This title was to remain unchanged until the formation of the Port of London Authority in 1909, though in the meantime additional docks had been added to the existing system including the Albion Dock (1860) and Canada Dock (1876). In addition a new entrance at Lavender Dock was opened in 1862. Thus developed the Surrey Commercial Docks, as they were to be remembered for decades to come, which almost completed the apparently chaotic layout of timber docks in Rotherhithe, although there was to be further construction after the turn of the century.

————————

The first of the new enclosed docks to be constructed during this period was the Victoria Dock. The building of this dock was enabled by Act of Parliament in 1850 (no monopolies), which sanctioned the Victoria Dock Co to create a dock on the western part of Plaistow Marshes, between Gallions Reach and Bugsby's Reach, again on the left bank, across part of a peninsula of land. This was duly opened in 1855 by Prince Albert. Entrance locks at the western end were 80ft wide and allowed ships of up to 26ft draught to enter, and the dock itself was over three-quarters of a mile long with a straight quay on the south side, although the north quay gained a number of 'finger' jetties projecting into the dock, later removed. Land to the east of Victoria Dock, as far as Gallions Reach was also acquired — this was later to become the site of the Royal Albert Dock. The dock was at once a success, aided no doubt by the fee of one penny per week in lieu of dues in order to attract business in the early days. Within five years, over ¾ million tonnes of shipping per year had been handled. Warehouses and sheds were there in quantity. Thomas Brassey (1805-1870), the railway contractor, was closely associated with the dock construction.

The fact that the Victoria Dock was the first to have a railway link to what passed, at that time, for a national network, is a reminder that the steam age had well and truly arrived — in fact the Victoria Dock was the first to have its own 'on quay' railway lines. Steam was also being applied to cargo-handling equipment. Hydraulic machinery too was installed, supplied by Sir William Armstrong. The railway

Right:
Thames barges clutter up the Surrey entrance to Surrey Commercial Docks in the 1930s, a picture which had not changed for decades.
*PLA Collection,
Museum of London*

aspect of the docks is described in a separate section, though it is worth noting here that while St Katharine, London and Surrey Commercial Docks never had railway connections, all the others did, and relied on them to a great extent to move goods and passengers over the years.

The year 1864 was significant on several counts. The opening of the Victoria Dock caused problems for those further up-river, which began almost immediately to lose business to the new facility, so that the St Katharine Dock Co merged with the London Dock Co and then took over the Victoria Dock Co. The result was known as the London and St Katharine Docks Co — it is curious that the name 'Victoria' was not incorporated in the title, since the dock bearing that name was the new company's most attractive and, unarguably, most successful asset. This grouping represented a formidable combination in terms of meeting competition afforded by other docks.

Also, as has been related, 1864 was the year in which the Surrey and Commercial Docks Co was formed by amalgamation, though this only affected the dock system within Rotherhithe itself, and was not spread across a range of towns and areas.

The situation in London was again beginning to reach the stage where there were more facilities than trade offering — hence the mergers. It is more than strange, therefore, to find again in 1864, yet another enclosed dock

system promoted. The Millwall Freehold Land & Dock Co (originally known as The Millwall Canal Co, founded 1864) presented a Bill to Parliament to enable the construction of an L-shaped dock on the Isle of Dogs, between the West India Docks and Greenwich Reach. The object of the exercise was to cash in on the handling of cheap foreign grain following the development of free trade with repeal of the Corn Laws (Surrey Commercial also tried this, but it was not a success). Thus grain-handling equipment and storage facilities were provided. The new dock estate, with 36 acres of water, also incorporated a dry dock, 413ft long in the southeastern corner, believed to be the first to be constructed by a London dock company, though the Victoria Dock Co had authority by Act of Parliament to build one. The 80ft wide entrance to the new dock was at the western end into Limehouse Reach, almost opposite the entrance to Surrey Commercial's Greenland Dock.

Millwall Dock was opened in March 1868 and was reasonably successful. This dock company also initially offered low rates and other inducements to attract traffic, making matters generally worse for itself and other dock owners, though it was good news for port users! Millwall Dock was never financially buoyant.

Although the West India Dock Co had bought the City Canal from the Corporation of the City of London in 1829, little was done in subsequent years except that part of it was widened for use as a timber pond. An Act to enable the company to convert the canal into a dock had been passed in 1831. The emergence of Millwall Dock doubtless provided the spur which encouraged the completion of South West India Dock (the former City Canal), which was effected in 1870 and which concentrated to a large extent on the handling of wool for which specially designed warehouses were provided, resulting in a loss of part of this trade by the London and St Katharine Co — which promptly fought back by improving its own facilities. South West India Dock was at a disadvantage from the start, since ships still had to use the old 45ft wide lock at Blackwall Basin.

Not surprisingly, there was now a pause in dock construction, though it lasted only a few years, and with hindsight one wonders why it did not stop there altogether. Although docks nearer the estuary clearly would have to come sooner or later, nobody in the dock companies seemed to have thought of developing the river banks down stream to handle bigger ships

faster (they would not have to spend time going through locks and manoeuvring towards and at the berth). There was a fixation about enclosed docks in the minds of the dock companies — obviously not shared by wharfingers — which was overcome only in the 1960s.

———————

The lull in dock building was shortlived. The London & St Katharine Dock Co felt the inevitable urge to fight back, particularly at Millwall's intrusion into its trades, and resolved to build the biggest and most impressive dock yet.

Below:
An early aerial view of Regent's Canal Dock. The canal itself can be seen stretching towards top right from under the railway arch.
PLA Collection, Museum of London

The P&O steamer ss *Rome* (1881), probably in the Royal Albert Dock. It is believed that this may have been her maiden voyage, and may also have been the first use of London by P&O as a passenger terminal. *P&O Group*

This new dock was to be built on land already owned by the company, between Victoria Dock and Gallions Reach, and the necessary Act was passed in 1875. It took five years to complete the project, which was opened by the Duke of Connaught, on behalf of Queen Victoria, in June 1880. It was named The Royal Albert Dock, the prefix 'Royal' being added to the name Victoria Dock at the same time, and is reputed to have cost £2.2 million. Facilities included 87 acres of water, a length of 1¾ miles, a depth of 27ft and, for the first time, electric lighting. Because of the increasing speed of cargo handling and the decrease in the time a ship spent in port, receivers and exporters handled their goods more quickly. Thus, warehouses were considered unnecessary, so that single-storey transit sheds were provided instead and served by road and rail. The architect for this prodigious scheme was Sir Alexander Rendel. It was said to be the largest enclosed dock in the world. The depth

at the entrance lock was 30ft, but competition from the proposed Tilbury Dock scheme caused the owners of Royal Albert Dock to open a second entrance immediately south of the first, which had a depth of 36ft and was in use by 1886.

The Royal Albert Dock immediately began to win general traffic from the India Docks and ships of up to 12,000 tons could be handled. Passengers became of increasing importance to port trade, and a railway link having been established with the Royal Albert Dock basin, Gallions Hotel was completed on the north side in about 1883. This was very convenient for passengers awaiting embarkation and for the families of ships' officers.

And so the tug-of-war between contending dock companies for the available traffic continued unabated. Revenues were falling and further mergers or takeovers were inevitable. Although serious efforts had been made to have the 'Free Water Clause' omitted from the new Acts of Parliament, these had failed, to the continued benefit not only of the lightermen but also to the increasing number of private wharves on the river banks (the

wharfingers), more of which had been granted sufferrence over the years. The abolition of the 'Free Water Clause' at this stage might have resulted in a very different state of affairs.

As it was, yet another scheme appeared. It was not particularly large, but it was certainly in a new place — Tilbury. This site was selected because, being opposite the principal arrival point at Gravesend where ships would wait at anchor for a suitable tide to enable them to proceed up-river (a time-consuming operation), it was thought that a dock built there would be bound to divert traffic away from the Upper Docks, and prosper. The East & West India Co came up with this project, spurred on by the completion of the Royal Albert Dock, which would involve the construction of a dock on a marshland estate some

Left:
In addition to the Tilbury Hotel, the dock company before 1910 provided a restaurant at the western end of the East Branch Dock, which catered separately for three classes of passenger. It finally closed in the 1970s. *Author*

Below:
Tilbury Dock much as it was when originally built. This view, taken some time later, is looking southeast over the entrance lock and Gravesend. *P & O Group*

450 acres in size and 26 miles down-river from London.

In July 1882 the necessary Act was passed in Parliament. It still held a 'Free Water Clause' though lightermen were reluctant to make use of it because of the distance from central London. The first sod was turned a few days after the Act was passed. But there was trouble with the contractors, Kirk & Randall, who were perhaps shortsightedly dismissed due to a combination of circumstances, one of which was their demand for a higher rate for handling blue clay discovered during the construction of the docks. It was a substance which proved difficult to work and delays ensued, but on 17 April 1886 the Tilbury Dock was finally opened when a Glen Line ship, the *Glenfruin*, arrived from China and entered the dock. Present at the formalities were the Lord Mayor of London and Sir Donald Currie, then one of the leading shipowners in Britain and head of the Union Line of Steamers to South Africa (later to become the well known Union Castle). Currie's ships regularly used London Docks, both then and for some time to come.

When Tilbury Dock opened it had practically everything. The water covered 56 acres, and there was an entrance basin of 19 acres, with a lock to the south, 695ft by 79.5ft. The depth of water in the entrance basin was 26ft minimum and in the dock itself 33ft — this was significant since it then enabled any ship to enter or leave Tilbury Dock at any state of the tide, clearly an advantage over all rivals. This dock, as others, was well supplied with cranes.

Houses were erected for officials, dock workers, foremen and police officers, and the prestigious 100-bed Tilbury Hotel was built

Above:
A sight reminiscent of the great days of commercial Thames sailing barges. *Spinaway*, (left), *Memory* and *Marjorie* lead a flotilla up-river. *Author*

Left:
The 1930s picture of P&O's *Strathmore* at Tilbury Landing Stage clearly shows the 100-room Tilbury Hotel, built by the dock company in 1886 and destroyed by bombing in about 1940. *P&O Group*

Above right:
Sailing ships predominate in this view of Western Dock, London Docks, in the 1890s, looking east. *PLA Collection, Museum of London*

ight on the riverside facing Gravesend, for the se of steamship passengers. Because an rrangement had been reached with the ondon Tilbury & Southend Railway, whereby ne latter would handle goods from the docks a new warehouse at Commercial Road, over 0 miles of dock company track was laid to all erths. Consequently, there was less need for arehousing, and few such were erected. In hort, when the dock opened everything was vailable; even lighterage was specially rranged, though this move did not materialise any great extent.

Even with all these advantages, in the initial ages Tilbury was a failure. After the first ush of enthusiasm it was little used and ould only attract traffic by quoting ludi-ously low rates. A year after opening, the ck company claimed that a great deal of usiness was being done, but at a price! The ast & West India Docks Co was in the hands receivers before the end of 1887. The dock stem was too extensive for the business ailable, in spite of the implications of the npire, and Tilbury Docks was the straw hich broke the camel's back. Both the

Millwall and the London & St Katharine Docks Companies reduced rates to compete with Tilbury (only Surrey Commercial was reason-ably successful during this time), so that, in the event, no one on the north bank was returning dividends. Consequently, in 1889 East & West India Dock Co and the London & St Katharine Dock Co entered into what was intended to be a mutually beneficial working arrangement, resulting in 1901 in a total amalgamation and the formation of the London & India Docks Co. Finally, by 1902 the following situation obtained:

● The Surrey Commercial Dock Co: control-ling all the Rotherhithe docks;
● The Millwall Freehold Land & Dock Co: Millwall Docks;
● The London & India Docks Co: East and West India Docks; Tilbury; London Docks; St Katharine Dock; Royal Victoria Docks; and Royal Albert Docks.

On the face of it, the last named of the three was in the strongest position, and in theory could have taken over the others. But local feelings ran too high for this ever to be a possibility. In 1900 the Surrey Commercial Co extended and deepened Greenland Dock, giving it an entrance lock equivalent in size to that of the Royal Albert (550ft by 80ft). The engineer on this project was Sir John Wolfe-Barry (1836-1918), who was already engaged in the construction of Tower Bridge when his advice was sought for the Greenland Dock project. The extended dock was opened for business in 1904 — but by then timber shipments had fallen off and even the Surrey Commercial Dock Co, buoyant so far, began to feel the pinch.

The situation had by now become so severe that a Royal Commission to look in particular into the financial and operational situations of the various enclosed dock companies was set up in 1900. Both wharfingers and lightermen were now united in opposing any watering-down of the 'Free Water Clause'. Not only were the dock companies competing with each other but they were also competing with the wharfingers — but this particular battle was heavily weighted in favour of the wharfingers. By the turn of the century, it was estimated that over 80% of all imports handled in the enclosed docks was being discharged direct to lighters for on-carriage to importers' premises or to private wharves — and dock companies received no revenue on these cargoes. Another problem which arose at this stage was that of navigational facilities: it was of little use to the Royal Albert Dock to have an entrance lock with a depth of nearly 30ft of water, when the navigable channel in Gallions Reach was only 18ft deep. Thus several features of the port needed looking at closely.

Yet, London was still the world's leading port. It had handled more cargo by both weight and value than any other port in the United Kingdom. By the turn of the century all major shipping lines were using it for services to and from destinations worldwide. Local traffic too was increasing. Passenger services and excursion trips proliferated, and the importation coastwise (mainly from Tyneside) of coal for the ever-hungry power stations and gas works had attained high levels — indeed by 1870 there was already in excess of four million tonnes per annum arriving in the Thames. A number of shipping companies made the Thames their home — names, many of which are long forgotten, like General Steam founded in 1824, or, are still with us, like F. T. Everard & Sons, and arguably Britain's largest privately-owned shipping company.

It is interesting to note that when the Royal Commission heard witnesses, it was said that London had become inefficient and was therefore losing trade to other ports. Some people would say that still applied in 1980. Glasgow, Liverpool and Hull were cited as examples, and it was claimed that by 1901 Liverpool's traffic was almost the same as London's, in terms of value. Another worrying factor, again, shades of criticisms to come, was that continental ports such as Antwerp and Rotterdam were expanding faster, and providing what the customer wanted better than London.

The Commission finally published its findings in the middle of 1902: quite simply, single, unified, public authority should run the docks, act in the interests of all port users and provide whatever navigational facilities were considered necessary. It was a tall order! The government itself, agreeing with and acting on these recommendations, placed a Bill before Parliament in 1903. But puerile argument was the order of the day — the Bill was simply ignored, and antagonists were given time to marshall their lines of battle. Notwithstanding all difficulties, the Bill finally became law on 21 December 1908.

The Port of London Authority, with all its responsibilities and ramifications, was born. But the private wharves were not to emerge unscathed. Only the lightermen maintained something like their traditional freedoms.

Below:
An assortment of sailing craft in the Lower Pool in about 1900. *Museum of London*

Strangers in the Port

Above:
In 1948 the passenger ship *Venus*, built in 1931, made a promotional visit to London which also took in Copenhagen and Oslo. Cocktail parties were held on board for special guests. She is seen here leaving on 1 May for Newcastle, to take up North Sea crossings. Eagle Steamers' *Royal Eagle* is on buoys to the left of the picture. *Author's Collection*

Below:
Built in 1931 for Red Funnel services from Southampton, *Medina* was sold to Bland, Gibraltar, in 1962 and renamed *Mons Abyla*. After changing hands further, she became a club house in 1977 at Brighton Marina, having the name *Medina* once again until moving to London. She is now a floating restaurant in the Export Dock (West India Docks). *Author*

Right:
The French Railway's car-ferry *Cote d'Azur* seen alongside HMS *Belfast* (the PLA's prestige berth) when she visited London in December 1981 for the World Travel Exhibition held at Olympia.
John F. Hendy

Below:
The *Celtic Surveyor* berthed in the Import Dock, West India Docks, serves as an Underwater Museum. She was better known as the *Earl of Zetland*, dating from 1939, which used to serve the outer isles of Shetland until being sold in 1975 for ocean survey work. *Author*

Bottom:
The Natural Environment Research Council owns and operates a number of ocean research vessels, including the RRS *Charles Darwin*, built in 1984 and seen here visiting the Thames in 1985. *Author*

IV

The Port of London Authority is Born and the Aftermath 1909-1964

By way of explanation — the year 1964 has been selected as the closing date for this chapter because the Port of London as a whole handled more cargo, 61.3 million tons, than at any other time. Further, the PLA enclosed docks in this year reached their peak in respect of cargo passing over the quays at the Royals, India & Millwall Docks and London & St Katharine Docks, as compared with previous years. In the meantime, tonnages at Tilbury and Surrey Commercial were rising. After 1964, tonnages began to fall and closures of all systems — except Tilbury — followed.

Below:
Four P&O liners in Tilbury, 1952. From the top:
Himalaya, Strathaird, Strathnaver and, probably,
Chitral. A London and Overseas' freighter is leaving
through the old locks.
PLA Collection, Museum of London

That year, therefore, marked the turning point in the fortunes of the Port of London Authority itself.

Arguments for and against the formation of a single authority raged for some time prior to 1908. There were several suggestions to the effect that the riverside wharves should be up-graded at the expense of the enclosed docks. This might have been a good idea, though with the amount of cargo passing through the port at the time, it was clearly impractical. Even with the passage of time it could not have been achieved without massive financial outlay, and it is doubtful if anyone could have raised sufficient funds. However, the President of the Board of Trade at the time, David Lloyd George, favoured enclosed docks

and it was his successor, Winston Churchill, who eventually caused the Port of London Act (1908) to appear on the statute book.

The board of the new company comprised some 28 members (though this number was to fall in later years), some of whom were nominated and some elected, representing various bodies with interests in the operation of the port. Areas of responsibility were clearly laid out.

Although the 'Free Water Clause' remained, the PLA was authorised to license barges, lighters and similar small craft (a right transferred from the Watermen's Company) and to raise a fee for registration. The PLA had the responsibility of controlling the Thames from Teddington to a line drawn between Haven Point (on Havengore Creek) in Essex and Warden Point in north Kent. Interestingly, ships using the Medway ports had to pass through the PLA's area and be subject to its regulations even though the Medway had its own navigational rules and pilotage. This still applies.

Other duties imposed on the PLA were the provision of approach channels of adequate depth, of barge and ship mooring points, and the licensing of riverside wharves which projected below the high water mark into the water — indeed as far as the last point was concerned, the PLA had the right to buy any riverside private wharf or warehouse by compulsory purchase. Wreck disposal, towage within the docks, surveying and, most important, operation of the enclosed docks, were all the PLA's responsibility. It was a daunting prospect for those concerned! Only three basic elements of port operation remained in other hands (apart from such as river towage): pilotage and lights were to continue to be maintained by Trinity House (incorporated by charter granted by Henry VIII in 1514); river police patrols were provided by the Metropolitan Police, Thames Division, which dated from 1839 (although its predecessors originated in the 1790s); and the Health Authority was still the City of London Corporation. Finally the PLA took over the responsibilities of the Thames Conservancy Board.

The financial situation of the Authority was, basically, to raise revenue through statutory powers by charges on ships using the port, on cargoes handled and stored, and other services provided for ships, importers and exporters, and anyone else who used its facilities. Out of this revenue, the first consideration was the payment of the cost of providing the port services and of the annual interest on the loans

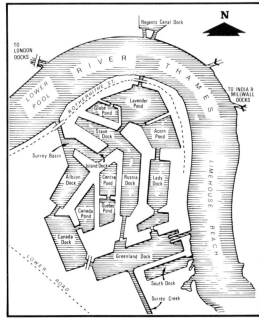

and the stock. Anything left over was to go t the port improvements.

During the period 1903-08, when Parliamen was playing table-tennis with the Port o London legislation, it was hardly surprisin that the existing independent dock companie were reluctant to invest to any great exten However, apart from improvements to Green land Dock already mentioned, it is wort noting that extensive grain silos were con structed on the south side of the Royal Victori Dock and at Millwall Dock. Naturally, the were competing. The Surrey Commercial Doc built cold stores. All these projects wer successful for varying lengths of time. It i worth remembering that not only were th dock companies competing with each othe but also with the private wharves. Before and during this period of relative stagnation on the part of the former, riverside wharves had been developing fast, so that by 1909 there were nearly 300 of them. Daunting competition for the Port of London Authority! In fact, a number of private wharves had already reached pre-eminence. Notable among these were Hay's Wharf (dairy products and other provisions), Butler's Wharf — including St Saviour's Dock (fruit, foodstuffs, spices), Irongate and St Katharine Wharves (used by General Steam for general cargoes from the continent and,

sometimes, the Mediterranean) — and so on. The fact of the matter was that during the latter half of the 19th century, private wharves grew in proliferation along both banks of the river mostly in a downstream direction from London Bridge. Tower Bridge, which had been opened in 1894, was never any obstacle to shipping which needed to use wharves in the Upper Pool. In fact, even since the early 1960s importers of dairy products, such as Empire Dairies and Dairy Produce Packers, still had properties in Tooley Street, and Hay's Wharf provided the discharging facilities for the 'beer and butter boats' from Denmark and elsewhere. But we digress.

Left:
Surrey Commercial Docks c1906.

Below left:
Checking tortoiseshell at a warehouse in St Katharine Dock in the 1920s.
PLA Collection, Museum of London

Below:
Gauging wine at London Dock in 1920.
PLA Collection, Museum of London

When the PLA came into being on 1 March 1909, it immediately inherited the dock systems owned by its predecessors, namely St Katharine, London, Surrey Commercial, East and West India, Millwall, the 'Royals' (Victoria and Albert) and Tilbury. In all, these dock

estates covered nearly 3,000 acres and included a total water area of some 700 acres, lengthy stretches of quay and railway track, four dry docks and ancillary equipment. Another problem facing the PLA at this time was that of labour relations. There had been, and would continue to be, strikes for various reasons, usually over pay. Labour was still being taken on a casual basis, and over 50 years were to pass before 'de-casualisation' became a reality, even though the PLA was under pressure to alter the system from the start.

As soon as the new board met, plans were evolved to carry out certain improvements with immediate effect, including dredging, the installation of a new pumping station at Gallions to increase the level of water in the 'Royals', improvements to Millwall Dry Dock and Western Dock at London and the construction of a new berth at Tilbury. Most important was the project for adding to the Royal Albert Dock, by building another dock parallel to it, on the south side. This was to be capable of handling ships of up to 30,000 tonnes, and was to total 64 acres. Plans were submitted in 1911 by Frederick Palmer, accepted and acted upon the following year — but the outbreak of war in 1914 was to prevent further development in this respect. Another move of significance was the pooling of the various dock companies' police forces into a single overall unit. In these early days the PLA returned a profit.

World War 1, conducted mainly — but not entirely — without air attack by either side, was initially beneficial to the port. London gained when Antwerp, Rotterdam and others were out of use. The number on the dockers' payroll had reached some 8,000 by 1915 (the usual number being about 4,500). But these balmy days were not to continue. The German U-boat campaign was successful from 1917 in discouraging shipping from using London, and from mid-1915 air strikes did occur, though unfortunately it was housing which suffered rather than the docks. Otherwise trade continued much as before, although essentials rather than luxuries became predominant.

When the war was over, the PLA embarked almost immediately on a massive spending spree, almost £20 million being committed to a variety of projects, for it was a boom era. The so-called Albert Dock Extension was opened by George V on 8 July 1921 and given his name. The dock itself was nearly as long as the Royal Victoria Dock (about ¾ of a mile) and was over 700ft wide at the eastern end, and 500ft at the other end. The double lock entrance had a basic total length of 800ft and a width of 100ft (the length could be extended), and could take ships of up to nearly 45ft draught. A feature of this dock was the provision of dolphins along the south side, away from but parallel to the quay. The space between them could be used by lighters and barges so that cargo could be discharged simultaneously to the quay, to lighters on the nearside and to lighters on the outside. At this early stage the depth of the approach channel to the Royals was not sufficient to take the largest ships, but a programme of dredging completed a few years later solved this problem. In the meantime the PLA's new central office building overlooking the Tower of London (known as the 'Wedding Cake'), was opened by the Prime Minister David Lloyd George, in October 1922.

It was during this period that the cargo jetty at Tilbury riverside was constructed, linked by rail to the rest of the system in the dock, while Tilbury Dock itself was extended to cover 9 acres from its original 74 acres. Further cold-store and grain facilities were provided at the Royal Albert Dock. On the riverside petroleum products grew in importance, with

installations at Purfleet and Thames Haven expanding rapidly. The postwar boom was not to last much longer. Tonnages fell off rapidly, in both imports and exports, a situation made worse by the General Strike of May 1926. It did not last long, but the docks were at a complete standstill (apart from what troops and volunteers could do) — a situation which was to arise several times in the future. Ernest Bevin is perhaps best remembered for his work on behalf of the dockers in these difficult times.

Nonetheless, some development did take place in the late 1920s, notably in the Surrey Commercial Docks, where Quebec Dock was opened in 1926, while two years later Lavender and Acorn Ponds were equipped with berths and sheds. At about the same time the Millwall and West India Dock systems, hitherto totally separate, were linked by a cut so that the entire dock system became interconnected.

In 1929-30 three new features appeared at Tilbury which were to strengthen its attraction to existing and potential users considerably. The original entrance having been found

wanting in size, a new one was opened at the southwestern end of the main dock in September 1929. This was to be the largest in the port and measured 1,000ft long, 100ft wide and with a depth at high water of nearly 50ft. It was capable of accommodating the largest ships at the time. At about the same time, the depth of water in Tilbury Dock itself was dredged to 38ft. A drydock, known as the 'New Drydock', was constructed in the southeastern corner of Tilbury (near to the original entrance) which was 750ft in length and is now the only one in the Port still operational. Finally a new passenger terminal was opened at Tilbury Riverside in May 1930 by the Prime Minister, Ramsay MacDonald. Sanction for its construction was granted by the passing of the Port of London and London and Midland Railway Act of 1922. Deep-sea passenger traffic through the port had been running at a level in excess of 300,000 per annum, and it was considered necessary to provide a central, convenient, embarkation and dis-embarkation point, with comfortable waiting areas and the inevitable Customs and baggage halls. The terminal was constructed by the PLA in conjunction with the railway, which built a new station alongside — still standing and magnificent in its way, though little used now and somewhat dusty. The landing stage consists of a platform 1,142ft long and 80ft wide, built on 63 pontoons. The first ship to use it was P&O's *Mongolia*, which arrived on the same day, shortly after the official opening. In spite of this facility, many passenger and cargo lines continued to use the 'Royals' and Tilbury enclosed dock to take on or disembark passengers, as well as the new landing stage. From now, for some considerable time, there was little investment, though money was spent in 1936 in the removal of the finger jetties in the Royal Victoria Dock so as to provide instead a continuous cargo-handling quay of

some 1,300yd. The increasing size of ships had rendered the original jetties redundant.

Although the 1930s were years of depression, activity in London was maintained at a steady level for the most part. That is to say, ships still came and went on their liner trades, though the amount of cargo they traded and discharged declined — for a time — and the sailings were less frequent.

It is useful at this stage to see who was using London during these years, and what cargoes they were carrying.

Traffic to the river wharves consisted mainly of coal to power stations and gas works, for which the various undertakings had their own colliers. Most of these were managed by Stephenson Clarke, supplemented as necessary by others taken on charter from such as France, Fenwick, Hudson and Comben Longstaff. Small tankers were also a common sight, bringing fuels into upriver tank farms and storage depots. Other wharves received cargoes of grain, timber, paper products, foodstuffs and general cargoes. By the mid-1930s private wharves had spread down river as far as Gravesend, with green fields here and there.

As far as the enclosed docks were concerned trade to St Katharine, London and East India Docks was by now virtually restricted to small coastal ships trading UK coastwise, to the Channel Islands and to northern Europe and occasionally the Mediterranean. Ships owned by the Coast Lines Group were prominent, as were those of General Steam. East India Dock though, was still talking in small liner cargo

Below:
P&O's *Mongolia* was the first ship to use the Tilbury Passenger Landing Stage when it was inaugurated in May 1930. *Ian Allan Library*

ships operated, for example, by Blue Star and Ellerman. There was considerable lighterage traffic bringing in goods typical to London and St Katharine, simply because of the specialist storage warehouses. These included coffee, spirits, tea and wines, as well as durables such as ivory, perfumes and wool. Guinness ships were well known!

The Surrey Commercial Docks were home to a number of well known lines, apart from the regular charter timber shipments. Greenland Dock, the largest, will be remembered particularly for the sight of Cunarders and Canadian Pacific, engaged in the St Lawrence trades. Apart from timber, dairy produce and grain were also handled in quantity, these trades being almost entirely North American orientated. In the West India and Millwall Docks, even now much of the cargo handled came from the Indian sub-continent, while grain was important to Millwall itself, often being carried in sailing ships. Cutler Street warehouse was still in use, as was that at Commercial Road, and was to remain so for some time to come, handling such high value goods as carpets, drugs, ostrich feathers and wine.

The Royal Group of Docks was by now extremely busy, and host to most of the well known lines of the day, many of which had their regular berths, often for passengers as well as cargo. Frozen meat was an important commodity, and special sheds and handling equipment were provided at Nos 29-33 Berths. The stevedores, Scruttons Ltd, were involved in this trade, particularly from South America. Scruttons had been earlier shipowners and stevedores in London since 1802. Until very much later, the PLA was not the sole employer of labour within the docks, there being a number of private companies which were

Above:
Wines being discharged in Millwall Dock in 1919.
PLA Collection, Museum of London

Below:
Unloading coffee in the West India Dock in the 1950s. Sacks are hung out to dry.
PLA Collection, Museum of London

41

contracted to various shipping lines. Among these, Scruttons was pre-eminent. Lines regularly using the Royal Albert were Atlantic Transport, British India, Brocklebank, Houlder, Lamport and Holt, Nelson, New Zealand Shipping and Messageries Maritime (French), believed to have been the first foreign line to have its own office in London, opened in Fenchurch Street in about 1890, and the Japanese Nippon Yusen Kaisha. Blue Funnel, Commonwealth, Cunard, Glen Line, P&O, and White Star were frequently seen in the King George V Dock, while the Royal Victoria handled Blue Star, Highland, Prince and Royal Mail, among others. However there was no particularly clear distinction and lines often used berths in other docks. At Tilbury, most commonly seen were ships of Anchor, Bibby, Brocklebank, Clan, Ellermen, Harrison, Orient, P&O — and so on. Many names, of course, have long since faded, though most were to last to at least the mid-1960s.

Below:
The Shadwell entrance to London Dock in the 1930s. As usual, lighters are prominent.
PLA Collection, Museum of London

The Port of London was never a cross-channel port of any significance, simply because the crossing was rather too long. However, short-sea passengers were being carried coastwise to such places as Leith, Tyneside, Plymouth, Ireland and Liverpool, from the upper docks. The Coast Lines Group was predominant in these trades. By the early 1930s the New Medway Steam Packet Co was running summer day excursions from Gravesend to Boulogne, Calais and Dunkirk, which were continued by Eagle Steamers after it took over the New Medway Steam Packet Co in 1936, but these could hardly be said to

constitute a 'cross-channel service' as such.

The shortest regular service to carry passengers was probably that offered by the Batavier Line between Rotterdam and London. It is believed that this was the first foreign concern to operate into London, a line which started regularly in 1830, and which was maintained

Below:
Gravesend Reach in about 1930, showing the Tilbury car-ferry *Mimie*. The other ship is probably *Batavier II* operated by Batavier Line between London and Rotterdam for cargo and passengers from 1921 to 1957. *PLA Collection, Museum of London*

Above:
The mv *Heron* was one of several motorships taken into the General Steam fleet in the 1930s for continental services from London. *P&O Group*

rather than the 'cross-channel' notion of sea travel.

---

right through until the late 1950s, although services were discontinued during World War 2. The Batavier Line was actually started by the Netherlands Steamship Co, but it was sold to Wm. H. Muller & Co in about 1896. Sundry river berths were used in the early stages, until the company opened its own wharf near Custom House Quay. For passengers, several berths were used over the years, including Blackwall, Tilbury and Gravesend — the last from 1922 at West Street. After World War 2 until closure of the passenger service in 1957, Tilbury was again regularly used. Various ships were used on the service, the maximum carrying capacity being around 180 passengers. The cargo service continued for another 10 years or so.

An effort was made by the French company Angleterre-Lorraine-Alsace Soc Anon de Navigation (ALA), in co-operation with the LMS Railway, when in 1927 a nightly service was started between Tilbury (Tidal Basin) and Dunkirk. The service was operationally feasible, with two fast turbine steamers, but was not attractive to the general public, and was transferred to Folkestone in 1932.

Passengers were also carried on certain other lines, such as cargo services operated to Denmark, by the United Steamship Co (now better known simply as DFDS), and to the North Baltic by the United Baltic Corporation, but they were verging on the 'long-distance'

Thus, quietly, during the 1930s trade continued, but volume fell. Investment in new equipment was limited to what was really needed. Most of the ships in the port carried the British flag, and the links of Empire were not yet lost.

Then came World War 2, which was to change everything. The Port of London Authority premises were to suffer over £13 million-worth of damage, since they and the river wharves were in the front line. Inevitably trade fell off, shipping being subject to the deprivations of enemy aircraft, mines, submarines and surface craft. The convoy system helped, but coastwise convoys suffered considerably. Control of Thames maritime movements was established at Southend Pier head. Shipping was sent to other ports, and not unnaturally, trade fell quite quickly to about quarter of what it had been in the late 1930s.

As far as the docks themselves were concerned, the starting date of the Luftwaffe bombardment is well documented. Saturday afternoon, 7 September 1940 was the day some 400 enemy aircraft arrived over the docks and caused complete havoc. Only Tilbury escaped. Surrey Commercial Docks blazed from end to end where nearly 250 acres of stored timber was lost, while most other docks received their quota of bombs, both high explosive and incendiary. Even the PLA Head Office in Trinity Square was hit. The bombardment is

reported as having continued for some 57 nights. Damage to buildings can be repaired at a price, but the sufferings of people in the areas of Wapping, Rotherhithe, Millwall *et al* cannot now be imagined. Evacuation led to the splitting of long-term friendships, and even families, so that the old camaraderie of dockland people began to disappear. Towards the end of the war those still living in these susceptible areas were subject to the silent horror of the flying bombs and V2 rockets. These must have been psychologically damaging, yet the people held on and continued to attend factories and docks to keep industry and commerce moving. They must have had nerves of iron.

On the other hand, it should not be thought that activity on the Thames came to a standstill. Far from it. In preparation for the return match of the D-Day landings, riverside and enclosed docks berths were busy constructing the PLUTO (Pipe Line Under The Ocean) equipment, which was to enable fuel to be pumped to Northern Europe for the use of the invading armies. The 'reels' for this pipeline were constructed at Tilbury. Most of

Above:
Further fire damage in the enclosed docks immediately after the 7 September 1940 raids.
PLA Collection, Museum of London

Below:
'Mulberry' pontoons being constructed in the drained East India Dock in 1944.
PLA Collection, Museum of London

the 'Mulberry' artificial harbour installation — interconnecting floating pontoons — was built in East India Dock. Warships were repaired afloat, or dry-docked, on the Thames. The New Drydock at Tilbury was big enough for cruisers of the 'Belfast' class. The estuary towers, carrying anti-aircraft and anti-submarine defence equipment, known as Maunsell Towers, were built in the Surrey Docks and then towed to their respective sites where some still stand.

The Port's final wartime triumph came on and after the D-Day landings, 6 June 1944, by which time the entire river was geared up to supporting the Allied effort in France. On D-Day itself, it is reported, over 200 ships left the Thames in support, together with nearly 2,000 barges, most of them loaded in the docks. In this way the people and the Port of London contributed to the final victory.

———

After the war, with the 'national effort' already becoming a thing of the past, dock labour was restive. Casual 'calling on' was still basically the order of the day, and dock workers were decidedly unhappy with the situation. Between late 1945 and May 1955 there were over 35 strikes for one reason or another. Mechanisation was partly responsible. The war had changed many things, and inven-

One of the PLA's heavy-lift cranes, the *London Atlas*, loading buses for export in London Dock (Shadwell Basin) c1946. *PLA Collection, Museum of London*

As if there could be any doubt, the crate was clearly marked 'Giraffe', when this cargo arrived in London Dock in 1946 for London Zoo.
PLA Collection, Museum of London

tiveness under need had resulted in equipment and the adoption of power to replace muscle going ahead faster than was acceptable to the dock workers of the time. Another factor which was to lead to changes was the growth of air travel, again instigated by the needs of the war machine, which resulted in a fall-off in passenger travel by sea, though this affected most ports, including Liverpool and Southampton, and not just London. Fork-lift trucks made their appearance for the first time, in a relatively primitive design compared with today's version, but still they were labour-saving devices. And this was the problem faced both by employers and employees. The former were keen to adopt the new equipment, the latter decidedly not! Another change wrought by the war and its aftermath was simply the loss to Britain of its Empire. The British merchant fleet was not to hold its own for much longer against rising 'nationalism' in overseas territories, though it

Above:
British India's *Chantala* enters King George V Dock as two barges moved outward. It is the early 1950s and there are not many empty berths.
PLA Collection, Museum of London

Right:
The Royals in about 1950. Royal Victoria Dock is at the top of the picture, with King George V Dock to the left and Royal Albert Dock to the right. A number of well known funnel markings can be seen, including British India, Bibby, Ellerman and Royal Mail. *PLA Collection, Museum of London*

continued to do just that until the early 1960s. What the fork-lift (or pallet-lift) truck had done was to remove the concept that cargo must be loaded and/or discharged in units which a man could handle. From now on, cargo could in practice be 'unitised' into far larger 'modules'. Another innovation was the ro-ro (roll-on/roll-off) idea. This, again, had been a wartime necessity, based on the tank and infantry landing craft. It was not long before 'containerisation' in its fullest sense appeared on the scene, but in the early 1950s it had hardly rippled the waters.

In dockland, war damage was gradually made good, and services initially reinstated on the prewar basis, although there were inevitably some changes. Britain tried hard to meet the requirements of the export market, but

with no notable success. In spite of all its difficulties, the trade through the Port of London was still the barometer for the trade of the United Kingdom as a whole and it began to pick up. All enclosed docks were back in business by the end of the 1950s although some like the St Katharine, on a much reduced scale, and most of the former familiar funnel colours were back. The passenger trade, apart from special emigration sailings, was not to approach its former level, thanks to the aircraft business, though some held on into the 1960s, notably Blue Star and P&O/Orient

Left:
General Steam's mv *Bullfinch,* **built in 1936, entering a quiet St Katharine Dock in the late 1940s. This small 194nrt ship rescued no fewer than 1,500 persons from the Dunkirk beaches on 29 May 1940.** *PLA Collection, Museum of London*

Below:
Atlantic Steam's *Empire Baltic* **was one of three similar ships which inaugurated the Tilbury-Hamburg ro-ro service in 1947.** *Author's Collection*

Right:
A well laden timber ship arrives in Greenland Dock entrance to Surrey Commercial for discharging in 1947. *PLA Collection, Museum of London*

Below right:
The wool warehouse with three-wheel articulated trucks and a steam crane in London Dock in the late 1940s. *PLA Collection, Museum of London*

among others. There was, by now, an even stronger imbalance of trade, so that by about 1960 imports exceeded exports by an alarming proportion. Another change during these years was the fall-off in goods carried by rail, and a massive increase in carriage by road, so that sooner or later the closure of the PLA's dock railway system was inevitable.

Nonetheless, the PLA tried to cater for new trades. Bulk wine was one of the more notable of these, with facilities being provided in the London Dock in 1959 — to be superseded not long afterwards by yet better facilities in West India Dock. Another important factor was that while trade with the Commonwealth fell, trade with Europe increased, but somehow London never seemed to come to terms with this — at least not at this time.

By the early 1960s the enclosed docks, as trade increased, began to look once again as they had done in the late 1930s. There was often no spare berth in the Royals or at Tilbury. On the riverside, new private wharves were developed, handling not just timber or aggregates or other specialised cargoes, but also 'third party' general goods and — later — container traffic as well.

Prior to the end of the period currently under review, only one dock had been closed. The East India Export Dock, small and very badly damaged, was filled in and sold about 1946. By 1956 the construction of Brunswick Wharf Power Station had been completed on the same site.

Early in 1959, a new building at Gravesend was nearing completion on a prime site overlooking the river and the stretch where estuary pilots and river pilots changed over. This was provided by the PLA to house the new Thames Navigation Service institution, which came into operation in May of that year. From now on, control of navigation on the river and in the estuary was based on one central point instead of being spread over a number of places as hitherto.

In Tilbury, where a new passenger terminal had been constructed in 1957 at No 1 Berth, mainly for P&O use, plans were already being made to extend the dock to cater for the increase in container movements, though they were a long time in reaching fruition.

In 1961-62 the bulk wine installation at No 23 Berth, London Dock, was expanded to take 530,000 gallons, while Cutler Street

Below:
Bullard King's *Umtata*, built in 1944, and Shaw Savill's *Dominion Monarch* discharge in King George V Dock, 1950.
PLA Collection, Museum of London

warehouse was provided with improved wine-bottling equipment. In Surrey Commercial Docks, Canada Dock was deepened, and the cutting between this dock and Greenland was improved to accept bigger ships. At this time, it cannot have been foreseen that the docks in question were going to fall into disuse so quickly.

The Port of London as a whole was gradually approaching what was to be its best year on record — 1964, when trade exceeded 61 million tonnes for the only time. It was also a year in which the number of enclosed docks reached its peak. From now on, it was to be a story of closures, redundancies and changes which were dramatic, thanks largely to 'containerisation', but London was not to lose its place as Britain's first port for cargo-handling.

Left:
The Thames Navigation building, completed in 1959, enabled movement control on the river and in the docks to be co-ordinated for the first time in one place. *Author*

Below:
Swedish Lloyd had a long association with London, for both passengers and cargo, until 1977. Here the long-lived *Suecia* built in 1929, is seen at Tilbury Landing Stage in 1962. *Author*

V

Decline of the Upper Docks and Developments at Tilbury 1964-1986

In 1964, the Port of London reached its peak in terms of tonnages handled. During the year, a total of 61,339,000 tons passed through the port. Of this total, 44.15% consisted of oils (there were and still are two refineries, and a number of tank farms). The PLA itself handled over its quays a total of nearly 2.4 million tons in the Royals, 1.1 million in India and Millwall, 0.75 million at Tilbury, 0.475 million in Surrey Commercial and nearly 0.4 million in London and St Katharine Docks. It is necessary to make a distinction at this point between tonnages handled over PLA premises. There is a big difference, and this is made up mainly of cargoes which were 'lightered' to and from ships. Thus, to take 1964 as an example, the total over PLA quays was 5.125 million tons, while the total through PLA stood at about 11.1 million tons, most of the difference going in lighters (5.975 million tons). The effect of the 'Free Water Clause' is immediately apparent!

Overall, it should be noted that in 1965

Right:
General Steam's motorship *Petrel*, built in 1945, signified the trend that appeared in small short-sea traders. She frequently traded to London.
P&O Group

Below:
Total Tonnages of Goods Handled — Port of London 1960-80; Analysis of Handling — Port of London 1960-80.

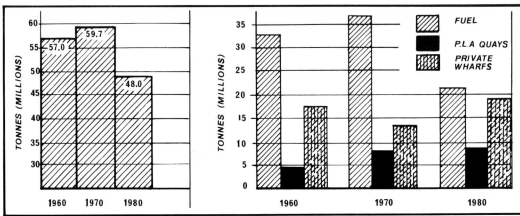

tonnages over PLA quays actually increased, thanks principally to improved figures at Tilbury and Surrey Commercial. Tonnages at the Royals, India and Millwall, and London & St Katharine fell, and were to continue doing so, as they were to at Surrey Commercial very soon afterwards.

1964 was a significant year in other respects. The Harbours Act was to extend the PLA's jurisdiction in the estuary by some 22 miles, to a new line between Gunfleet Old Light House in Essex to a point three miles northeast of Margate. By implication, this meant that even more extensive dredging had to be done, so it is hardly surprising that at this time the PLA owned and operated no fewer than seven dredgers and 14 hoppers. As an aside, it is interesting to note that at this time the PLA owned no fewer than six floating cranes, 583 quay cranes, 224 mobile cranes, seven floating grain elevators, 198 lighters, 24 dock and river tugs, nine salvage vessels, 11 conservancy vessels and seven survey craft!

It was in this year that the extension to Tilbury Dock was started, and the St Katharine Dock House was nearing completion. But passenger traffic was falling off as air travel improved, and a total of 181,520 passed over Tilbury Landing Stage, though this was to increase to more than 195,732 in 1965.

Over the next few years further improvements were made to the enclosed docks, and even with hindsight it must be said that the PLA was unwise in initiating some of these projects. London, Millwall and Surrey Commercial were subject to a number of schemes, while the Western entrance to the Royal Victoria Dock was in 1965 under reconstruction for the use of barge traffic. It was in this year when the enclosed docks as a whole handled more traffic than at any other time over their quays, the total reaching 5.162 million tonnes. In 1966, the bulk wine berth at London Dock was extended, this time to a capacity of 804,000 gallons. In July of this year Stage 1 of the Tilbury extension (Branch Dock) was opened for business, incorporating No 36-38 Berths specifically for trade with India and Pakistan. Other contemporary projects included a further extension of Tilbury Branch Dock (Stage II), the reconstruction of sheds in Millwall Dock (one of

Left:
A PLA responsibility is the clearing of driftwood from the river as well as the docks. The *Driftwood I* is in action here, with the extension added in 1985. *Port of London Authority*

Below:
Shaw Savill's *Doric*, built in 1949, was often seen in the Royals, trading with Australia in the 1960s. *Ian Allan Library*

which was for Fred Olsen's exclusive use for cargo and passengers), and further mechanisation of the Royal Victoria frozen meat facilities.

On a broader front, 1966 was notable not only for the initial development of the 'decasualisation' of dockers, but also for the passing in Parliament of the Docks & Harbours Act, which introduced licensing for the employment of registered dock workers — the PLA was designated as licensing authority for the Thames, and although it was not foreseen

at the time, this was to be the chain around the neck of the Authority in years to come. However, as far as the PLA was concerned, there were some who were looking ahead, for it was in this year that 12 straddle-carriers were ordered for the quayside handling of containers at Tilbury.

On the river itself, the North Thames Gas Board methane installation at Canvey Island became fully operational in 1965, and following extensive dredging in the approach channel, the largest tanker to berth in the

Left:
The new PLA river patrol vessel was officially named *Ravensbourne II* at the Tower Pier in February 1986.
Port of London Authority

Right:
Composition of Traffic Handled over PLA Quays — 1966-84 (including Tenant's Quays).

Below:
The *Amazon* was one of three Royal Mail Line sisters which served South America from the Royals for passengers and cargo from 1960. Their withdrawal in 1968 sounded the death-knell of the passenger connection.
Ian Allan Library

Left:
By 1965, Ellerman Wilson Line had replaced the *Borodino* on the London-Copenhagen passenger cargo service with the smaller *Aaro*, with accommodation for 12 persons only. *Author*

Right:
In September 1968 European Unit Routes (P&O Group) introduced the new *Impala* to services between Tilbury, Rotterdam and Dunkirk. This represented the modernised version of General Steam's conventional services.
Ian Allan Library

Thames up to that time, arrived at the Shell refinery at Shellhaven (also known as Thameshaven). She was the steam tanker *Seven Skies* (93,250 dwt) which brought in 89,000 tons of crude, on a draught of over 44ft. This record was to be broken towards the end of 1968 when Shell's *Megara* (210,000 dwt) arrived with a part cargo. Not to be outdone, the Mobil refinery at Coryton was looking for even bigger tankers, and work was started so as to enable ships of up to 200,000 dwt to use its berth on a part-cargo basis. Additional

moorings were provided by the PLA at Denton for petroleum barges.

In 1967, work continued on the enclosed docks, but by now the warning signs were plain for all to see. Use of the upper docks in particular was declining, so that the decision was taken to close St Katharine & London Docks within 12 months.

On the debit side of this year, the Surrey Lock entrance to the Commercial Docks was closed and filled in as was the western entrance to Millwall Dock where in-filling was

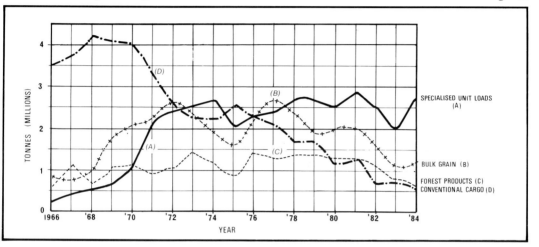

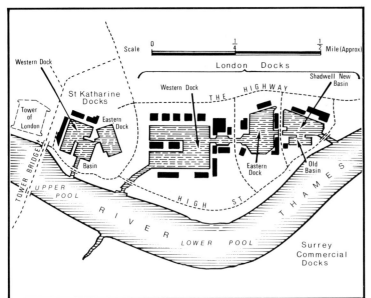

started. The upper entrance to the Royals at Gallions was also closed to shipping, as was the old southeastern entrance to Tilbury at about this time. On the credit side, Stage II of Tilbury's extension was gradually proceeding, and Nos 42 and 44 Berths became operational. Work started on the riverside grain terminal at Tilbury, and on the rail container terminal, in conjunction with British Railways.

Of particular significance during that year was that 'decasualisation' was implemented as from September, and that the PLA not only clarified its duty to register small craft on the river, but also was confirmed in its (later, unhappy) situation as 'employer of last resort' by reason of its responsibility for licensing the employment of registered dock workers, from 1 January 1968. In the long run, this meant that the PLA had to accept on to its pay-roll dock workers made redundant in the event of a licensed riverside wharf going out of business, which was to happen all too frequently in the years to come.

The run-down of the enclosed 'upper docks' started in 1968, though of course sometimes a considerable period elapsed between the departure of the last ship, and the closure of warehouses or the removal of the last piece of cargo. In practice, a dock is technically closed when the last import consignment had been collected, but it is virtually impossible to put a date to this activity. Over the next few years dramatic changes were to take place.

In 1968 both St Katharine and London Docks were closed, although the warehouses attached to the former remained in use for nearly another year, and the bulk wine facilities only recently expanded, continued to be served by road transport. East India (Import) Dock was also closed. In Surrey Commercial Dock, at the same time as some in-filling took place, notably at Lady Dock, incredibly new amenity blocks were being erected for dock workers, and some shipping lines displaced from London Docks were transferred there. Also in 1968, Millwall dry-dock was closed. In the following year, both Lavender and Norway Docks were being filled in and St Katharine was sold to the Greater London Council.

In the meantime, further new berths became available in the Tilbury extension, including Nos 40 and 43 Berths in 1968 and No 39 Berth in February the following year. The last was a specialised container berth to be operated exclusively by OCL and ACT, for the Australian trade. Unfortunately, lack of agreement or working arrangements with the dockers resulted in both the Rail Container Terminal and the berth remaining out of use until May 1970, the *Jervis Bay* (26,876 grt) making the first sailing on the 17th. The tenants of the timber terminal at No 46 Berth in the new extension, Seaboard Pioneer, were similarly affected by the lack of working agreements. However, during 1969, working arrangements were agreed at a number of existing and new berths, notably with Swedish Lloyd (No 2 Berth), Canadian Transport (Terminals) Ltd

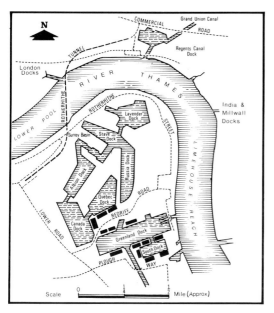

(No 42 Berth), SCA Sales Ltd (No 44 Berth), and at the PLA's own multi-user facilities at Nos 34 and 43 Berths.

In May 1969, the closure of London Dock was completed, and it was put on the market, although certain buildings were still used for a short time for storing goods like carpets and tobacco displaced from Cutler Street warehouse. The latter was sold to private devel-opers in January 1973 but the buyers were unable to finalise, and the property was put up for sale for the second time, the PLA retaining the buildings and the deposit! The property was finally sold in June 1978 again for private development. London Dock had been bought by the London Borough of Tower Hamlets two years previously. The magnificent head office building at Trinity Square was sold in June 1972, by now being far too big and expensive to run for the reduced staff required. It was at this time that the PLA also decided to sell the St Katharine Dock House (now the World Trade Centre), completed in 1965.

It is useful at this stage to follow through the story of dock closures, returning to developments at Tilbury later.

In the Surrey Commercial Docks, improvements carried out in the 1960s were irrelevant to the changing patterns of the timber trade. Bigger ships and the increasing growth of the packaging and palletisation of timber and timber products brought more trade of this kind to Tilbury and the riverside wharves at the expense of the Surrey Docks. Initial ministerial approval for the closure of the entire dock and canal system was secured by the PLA in April 1970, though in fact the

necessary legislation (Port of London Bill) was not enacted until December. Cargo services were almost completely phased out by September, by which time a further 15 berths were closed. By year-end it was all over, the last ship being the Russian timber carrier *Kandalakshales* (4,673 grt) which left on 22 December. The Russian services were transferred to the Royal Albert Dock, while others went to India and Millwall, and Phoenix Wharf.

By the middle of 1977, the Surrey Commercial 'estate' had been sold in sections to the London Borough of Southwark and the Greater London Council. The East India Dock (Import) section, which closed in 1968, was finally sold to the CEGB in 1971. It will be remembered that the Export Basin alongside had been sold, also to the electricity authority, some 20 years later.

In India and Millwall Docks, business in the late 1960s was still good, and a series of improvements was put in hand over the next few years. New sheds and a passenger terminal for Fred Olsen were planned at J, K and M Berths (Millwall Dock), which were completed by the end of 1969. During the same year work was finished on the development of bulk wine stores at Wood Wharf to hold 380,000 gallons, although the decision had

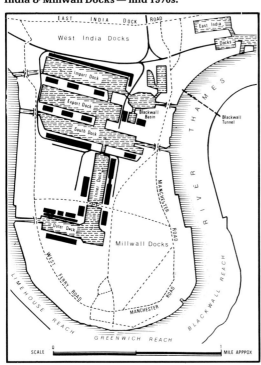

already been made to extend capacity by a further 600,000 gallons, following the start of the rundown at London Dock. Demolition of the central granary started in the Inner Dock (west side), while further amenity facilities were provided to accommodate a total work force of some 1,350 registered dock workers.

Between then and 1980, when India and Millwall Docks were closed, there was a curious combination of the closure of some berths and the upgrading of others. There were several notable changes during this 10-year period. In 1976, all bulk-wine handling was concentrated here, although the peak had already been reached two years earlier when a total of 9.6 million gallons were handled by both Garnet Street (London Dock) and India and Millwall. In 1978, six berths were closed, followed by others in subsequent years. A little earlier the decision had been taken to provide a special container berth in West India Dock, and a container handling crane was imported from the continent for this purpose in 1979, but never saw use due to industrial relations problems and it was later moved to Tilbury. Also in 1979, operational berths were reduced to 10 in number, and negotiations were opened with Telscher Brothers Ltd for the building of a wine bottling and storage plant next to the bulk wine facility, which was to have a total capacity of 80,000 cases per annum. This was opened in December 1980, although wine tankers ceased to use the berth in late 1983. Since then, cargoes have been discharged at Phoenix Wharf on the river, and then taken by road to Telscher's.

The announcement was made in March 1980 that the West India Dock complex was to close, and cargo-handling was to be transferred to the 'Royals' or Tilbury, excepting the bulk-wine facilities and Montague L. Meyer's timber operations. This was completed in the following July without any loss of customers — in fact, former users of the docks were said to have expressed themselves better pleased with the new arrangements, in the sense that cargo-handling was faster and therefore vessel turn-around was quicker. Fred Olsen had already moved to Tilbury in 1980, taking No 36 Berth where passenger and other facilities were provided, and Meyer's timber traffic moved to Tilbury in May 1983.

And so to the 'Royals', where, in the late 1960s and early 1970s trade was still running at a high level. This was partly due to the transfer of lines from enclosed docks further up-river. The construction of dockers' amenity blocks was still going ahead. In fact in 1970 a project was nearing completion which would

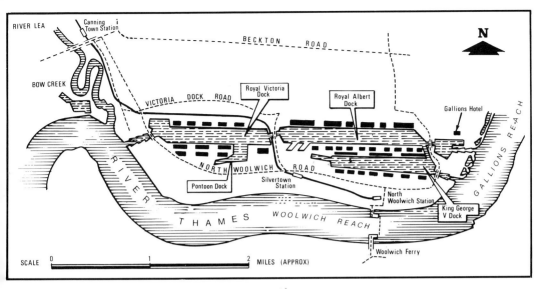

be able to accommodate 4,750 registered dock workers. But a new move by the PLA in this year was significant in its implications, thanks to the developing bulk grain terminals. This was the disposal of all the floating grain elevators. Another feature of the year 1970 was the closing of all PLA railway operations, where they still survived, although rail connections with BR were maintained at the container terminals, and at the 'Royals'' heavy-lift facility. In succeeding years, though, a number of berths were closed — the drift by now being very definitely towards containerisation, for which the 'Royals' were not sufficiently well-equipped.

By 1979, the number of operational berths in the Royal Group had been reduced to 10, and the Royal Albert Dock Basin yacht marine project — initiated at great expense some years earlier — was terminated; no one was using it to any great extent.

A further nail in the coffin of the 'Royals' occurred in 1980, when the grain importers, Rank-Hovis and Dalgety-Spillers, situated on the south side of Royal Victoria Dock, ceased to take in supplies by water. Thus there was no further need for PLA stevedoring facilities which, consequently, were withdrawn. The silos still stand in isolated splendour. By the end of 1980, there were only seven berths operational in the 'Royals', based entirely on conventional trades (such as the Chinese, at Nos 31-33 Berths, and contract cargoes at No 7 Berth, all in the Royal Albert Dock).

Clearly, the days of the Royal Docks were numbered, although scrap metal had become of some importance here. George Cohen had already started handling this commodity and

plans were laid for Mayer, Newman to follow suit. In fact, in October 1981 the handling of all liner trade conventional cargoes ceased in the Royal Docks, those which were left being transferred to Tilbury. The last ship to discharge cargo was the Chinese *Xingfeng*, which completed on 26 October. There was no loss of traffic on the transfer to Tilbury, which took only two or three weeks to finalise. The scrap metal business was moved to Tilbury in June 1983, after which time the 'Royals' were used only for laid-up shipping, which proved to be a mixed blessing for the PLA. While it was true that revenue was being earned, expenses were also incurred by the cost of maintenance and security staff. The last movement in the 'Royals' took place in November 1985, when an assortment of tugs, barges and the former Clyde-built liner *Queen Mary*, undergoing alterations for use as a river restaurant, 'locked-out' through the King George V Dock entrance at Gallions Reach. By this time, the Royal Victoria Dock area had been sold to the London Docklands Development Corporation, which, early in 1986, leased 476 acres of the Royal Albert and King George V Docks.

Over the years, while the upper docks of necessity were being run down, the PLA was developing Tilbury at a commendable rate. It cannot be said that it was slow in this respect. Mention has already been made of the

expansion of the dock itself, of the provision of container berths and of handling equipment. Indeed, Tilbury, in the early years of containerisation did very well, not only with containers, but also with ro-ro traffic and with conventional cargoes in those trades where they were still required.

Money was spent to good effect, starting in 1969, when the riverside grain terminal became operational in June. In spite of problems with the silos, about 850,000 tonnes of grain was handled by the end of the year. As has been mentioned above, the OCL-ACT container berth (No 39) and the Rail Container Terminal both became operational in May 1970. Initially two shifts were available here, but from October, round-the-clock working was offered seven days a week, bank holidays included. Also during this year, a second Goliath crane was ordered for the Rail Container Terminal, and more straddle-carriers introduced to these container berths.

At this time, the PLA still had the responsibility of maintaining the various dry docks situated in the 'Royals' and at Tilbury. Millwall had already been closed, and at the end of 1970 only three remained — two at the 'Royals' and one at Tilbury. All three the

Left:
The Tilbury Docks as they are today, after all extensions had been completed. Note the drydock in the bottom left and the riverside grain silo in the top right. *Port of London Authority*

Below:
British Waterways' Regent Canal Dock: trans-shipping cargoes to and from barges. By 1969 this activity had virtually ceased. *Ian Allan Library*

following year were used by a consortium known as River Thames Ship-repairers' Association following nationalisation of most of the ship-building and repairing industry. Eventually this collapsed, so that only the 'New' dry dock at Tilbury was now in use.

Also in 1970 the PLA introduced a piece of paperwork, innovative at the time, but which was quickly adopted by port authorities the length and breadth of the country. This was known as the 'Standard Shipping Note', on which details of an export consignment were entered. It was introduced on 1 April for a trial period, and it was so successful that it was made compulsory in the port from 30 June 1970. Now, every forwarding agent is familiar with the document in its up dated form.

By 1972, Tilbury had become the leading container-handling port in the UK, attaining 231,438 boxes. This figure also gave it second

Right:
The CEGB-owned, but Fisher-managed, heavy-lift ro-ro ship *Aberthaw Fisher* **loading transformers for Hamburg at No 4 Berth, Tilbury, in 1979. This berth was specially equipped for cargoes of this kind.** *Author*

Below:
On 22 July 1969, the New Zealand Shipping Co's *Rangitoto* **disembarked passengers at Tilbury Landing Stage for the last time, whereupon the passenger service to and from New Zealand ceased.**
Ian Allan Library

lace in Europe. In that year, eight new lines
tarted using the multi-user container berths,
ncluding Hapag-Lloyd (to US East Coast),
ombi Line (South America and US Gulf),
ohnson Scanstar and Holland Steamship Co.
Iore were to come, but unhappily several
ere to move later to ports such as Felixstowe.
n 1972 the grain terminal had a record year
ith no fewer than 1.078 million tonnes being
andled.

1973 was also beneficial to Tilbury. Both the
ew West African Terminal at Nos 31-33
erths, and the ro-ro berth at Riverside close
the passenger landing stage were opened,
e former becoming operational in 1974. It is

Above:
**The *Maron*, a 21,310dwt combi-carrier, was the first
Ocean ship to be handled by Blundell and Crompton
in Tilbury Dry Dock, seen here in August 1985.**
Author

Below:
**The Swedish ro-ro ship *Jon Gorthon*, 8,350dwt,
arriving at Tilbury with forest products in August
1985, with the help of PLA tug *Platoon*.** *Author*

still in use for its original purpose and is used
mainly by UKWAL (West African Conference
Lines) Companies. The ro-ro berth has had a
somewhat chequered career, but is at the time
of writing in use for regular freight ro-ro

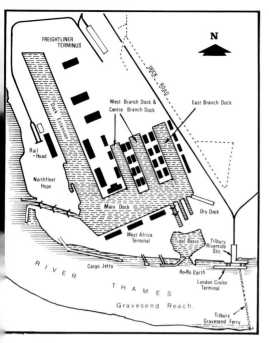

Above left:
Searoads Ferries' chartered Spanish ro-ro ship
Reina Del Cantrabrico, used on the Zeebrugge run
early in 1985. *Author*

Left:
SAECS—*Table Bay* discharging and loading at
Northfleet Hope (Riverside) Container Terminal in
1982. *Port of London Authority*

Above:
Tilbury Docks — 1980.

Below:
On 27 June 1982, the 50-seat Brymon Dash 7 made an
experimental landing on Heron Wharf in the West
India Dock.
London Docklands Development Corporation

service to and from Zeebrugge operated by
Searoads Ferries. At the container terminals,
Tilbury saw a throughput of 246,000 boxes
(about 287,000 teu's) and the importation of
forest products reached a peak of 1.23 million
tonnes.

It has been mentioned earlier that the PLA
was not the only employer of dock workers in
the enclosed docks in the past. However, an
inevitable result of the fall-off in trade and the
closure of docks was that independent
employers began to feel the pinch and
ultimately could no longer survive. In 1973 the
PLA took over the business of two of them,
Thames Stevedoring and Metropolitan
Terminals, followed in 1974 by Gee Stevedoring and the largest independent employer,
Scruttons', in April 1975. In February 1979
T. Wallis Smith Coggins closed down. From
now on, the PLA was the sole stevedoring
employer in the docks. But it will be
remembered that, under the terms of its
constitution, the PLA had to take all registered
dock workers thus out of work into its own
employ, creating an enormous surplus of
labour. By early 1976 therefore, there were far
more dockers than were needed, and the daily
surplus was in the region of 1,250 men — all
being sent home on pay!

It was in 1977 and 1978 that the drift of
deep-sea lines away from Tilbury began. In the
former year, Ellerman Harrison Container
Line, Lovell and Ben went, while in 1978
Harrison Line, which had used the West India
Dock since it opened in 1802, disappeared.
There were others. On the other hand the grain
terminal had another record year in 1977,
handling 2 million tonnes for the first time.
1978 saw the opening of the Northfleet Hope
Terminal — the first riverside container berth

to be provided by the PLA. Operated by tenants Tilbury Container Services Ltd, it opened for business on 9 September, and was used by TCS constituents OCL-ACT (A) and Canadian Pacific. Australian National also used it by special arrangement. The riverside berth itself is 305m long and there is a small freightliner rail-head. TCS therefore now operates both this berth and No 39 Berth inside the dock.

Two notable improvements were carried out at Tilbury in 1983. No 40 Berth was converted to full combi-capability, incorporating a clear-span aluminium shed covering 3.482sq m and both conventional and Paceco container cranes. The other improvement was the opening of Stage I of the new riverside export grain facility. Stage II being completed the following year.

To bring the story of Tilbury up-to-date, a number of other improvements is worth

Left:
The new Tilbury Custom House was operational from February 1985 and it is known as the 'Fire Station' because of its red bricks and red paintwork. For the first time, all branches of Customs' activities at Tilbury were able to be concentrated in one building. *Author*

Above:
The 35,055dwt *Nortrans Enterprise* was one of the largest ships to use No 13 Berth, seen in September 1985, when she loaded over 26,000 tonnes of scrap for China. *Author*

Right:
The PLA's multi-user container berths, 41-45, as well as the Tilbury Container Services Berth 39, are all fully occupied early in 1985.
Port of London Authority

Above:
**Nedlloyd's combi-carrier *Nedlloyd Everest*, built in
1973, takes on containers at the PLA multi-user 43
Berth, Tilbury, for India and Ceylon in 1985.** *Author*

Above right:
**By contrast a modern Nedlloyd cellular container
vessel *Nedlloyd Clarence* is loading for the Middle
East at 43 Berth. She was built in 1983.**
Port of London Authority

Right:
**Palm Line's *Lagos Palm*, built in 1982, was a regular
visitor to Tilbury's West Africa Terminal on the
conference lines service.** *Palm Line*

mentioning. The scrap terminals became
operational in November 1984, and the entire
straddle-carrier fleet was renewed by the
middle of 1985. The riverside passenger
terminal was refurbished and re-opened as the
'London Cruise Terminal' in January 1985. It
currently handles some 75 ships per year —
mostly CTC and Polish Ocean Lines. Tilbury
never stands still. In 1984, a total of 5.4 million
tonnes of cargo of all kinds was handled over
Tilbury quays (both PLA and Tenants'), of
which unit-load traffic comprised 2.7 million
tonnes, including 325,000 tonnes of container-
ised cargo. Bulk grain, at 1.2 million tonnes,
was the second largest commodity, followed
by forest products and conventional cargo,
each returning around 600,000 tonnes. Bulk
metal, mainly scrap, reached 300,000 tonnes.

On 17 April 1986, the Port of London
Authority celebrated the centenary of the
opening of Tilbury Dock. It enters its second
century with optimism. Most labour problems
have been solved, and the dock is well
equipped to support shipping of all kinds.
There are no fewer than 19 services to Europe
including the Mediterranean, for example, and
there are no continent and few principal
overseas ports which are not served from
Tilbury.

Port Railways

Right:
North Woolwich station was built in about 1856, to replace a wooden one constructed when the Eastern Counties Railway reached here in 1847. It was extremely busy at one time for goods and passengers, many of whom travelled over to Woolwich by the railway ferry. The station building was closed in 1970 in favour of a new one and is now a railway museum. *Author*

Below:
Hudswell Clarke 0-6-0T locomotive No 67 after repainting in the PLA's blue livery in the 1950s. Between 1956 and 1961, 44 steam locomotives were replaced by 27 diesels which continued to operate until all PLA rail operations ceased from 1 May 1970. *Chris Blamey*

Left:
Janus **one of the new 400hp PLA diesel engines produced by the Yorkshire Engine Company, crossing the 'New' Tilbury Lock entrance bascule bridge in the 1960s.** *Chris Blamey*

Below:
A Class 40 locomotive pulls away from its train of wagons at the Tilbury Freightliner Container Terminal, opened in 1969. There is also a units-terminal alongside the Northfleet Hope Container shipping complex, opened in 1979, and between them they handle about 67,000 containers each year.
Port of London Authority

Top:
A two-car EMU stands at North Woolwich station in 1985. There is a half-hourly service from here on the North London line via Stratford (Low Level), Gospel Oak and Willesden Junction (High Level) to Richmond. The engine alongside is a preserved Robert Stephenson & Hawthorn 0-6-0ST. *Author*

Above:
A new bridge over the West India Dock, Import Dock will carry the Docklands Light Railway 8m above the water. There are similar bridges over the Export Dock and South Section. *Author*

Right:
The Docklands Light Railway was built under Acts of Parliament as a joint scheme by the London Docklands Development Corporation and London Regional Transport. Two routes were due to open in July 1987: Tower Gateway-West India Quay-Island Gardens and Stratford-West India Quay-Island Gardens, with an extension planned from Tower Gateway to Bank. Unit 01, built by *GEC,* is seen on test in September 1986. *Brian Morrison*

VI

The Private Wharves and River Traffic (Postwar Years)

In previous chapters, reference has been made to the growth in importance of the private wharves, including those handling general cargoes, power stations, gas works and oil refineries. It is clearly impossible to give the full story of these undertakings in a book of this size and scope, but it is worth mentioning some of particular interest.

One of the largest single bulk commodities handled by the port over the years was coal, which was required for domestic use as well as for power plants. Many power and gas companies had their own fleets of colliers which were kept busy feeding the riverside plants, but it was during the 1960s when changes became significant, and tonnages handled began to fall from the level of about 14 million tonnes a year in the early part of the decade. The discovery and practical application of North Sea gas put an end to the production of gas from coal, some gas-works were closed altogether, and others converted

Above:
Beckton Gas Works was the largest in Europe when opened in 1868. All coal supplies were taken in by 'down-river' colliers until it closed in 1970.
British Gas

Below:
The mv *Falconer Birks*, a 'flat-iron' built in 1953, was the last of the North Thames Gas Board's fleet of colliers, and is seen here making the final delivery to Nine Elms Gas Works in January 1970. *British Gas*

Left:
West Thurrock Power Station, which opened in 1954, can burn either coal or natural gas and is still in use. *CEGB*

Below left:
One of the older Thames-side power stations was that at Woolwich, operational from 1901 to the 1970s. In this view c1968, Shipping and Coal Company's *Greenland*, built in 1962, is discharging coal. *CEGB*

Above:
The first of three 'super-colliers' of 19,000dwt to be delivered in 1985-86. This is the *Sir Charles Parsons*, which mainly serves West Thurrock and Tilbury 'B' Power Stations. *CEGB*

Below:
This view of the Nelson Drydock at Rotherhithe, photographed in the 1940s, shows Thames sailing barges moving up river, and Bulk Oil's *Pass of Hallater*, built in 1928, undergoing repairs aground'. *PLA Collection, Museum of London*

for storage purposes only. The transition was remarkably quick, from the first discovery off Grimsby in September 1965 and its acceptance as a fuel in 1966. The last Thames-side gas works to receive carbonising coal was Nine Elms in January 1970. When nationalisation became effective from 1 May 1949, the various collier fleets were absorbed by two main groupings, the South Eastern Gas Board (whose colliers had all been disposed of by the end of 1971) and the North Thames Gas Board (whose last, the *Falconer Birks*, was sold in 1970). Beckton Gas Works, the largest in Europe when it was constructed in 1868, was closed at about the same time.

As anyone who travelled down to the Thames not long ago will be aware, there were many electricity power stations, all of which were coal-fired initially. There can be few who

had not heard of Bankside, Battersea, Deptford, Fulham, Lots Road (built to supply the London Underground) and Tilbury, to name but a few. Most have now been closed. On nationalisation of the industry on 1 April 1948, the British Electricity Authority (London Division), as it then was, absorbed the fleets of Thames colliers formerly operated by the London Power Co Ltd, and Fulham Borough Council. The present name — Central Electricity Generating Board — came into use in 1958. When the old up-river power stations became uneconomical to operate, they were accordingly closed, and supply was concentrated in large modern stations down-river.

Above:
The 14,905dwt bulk carrier *Mananjary* discharging molasses at Tate and Lyle's Silvertown berth in August 1985. *Author*

Below:
Hay's Wharf in 1967: the DFDS ship *Naxos* is ready to leave after her 'beer and butter' run from Denmark. *Author*

Above right:
The ro-ro ship *Car Express* waiting to berth at Ford's, 1977. *Author*

Below right:
United Baltic's *Baltrover*, built in 1949, was the company's last conventional ship to carry passengers on the Baltic service. She is seen leaving the Pool in 1962. *Author*

Belvedere, due to close in October 1986, was opened in 1953, West Thurrock in 1954, Tilbury 'A' in 1958 and 'B' in 1965. The most recent — Littlebrook — came on stream in 1983. Of these, most are adaptable for the use of coal or oil, or even gas in some cases, so that the CEGB still needs colliers. But they are all different from the smaller 1,500-2,000 tonners which used to frequent the river, whether down-river conventional colliers or up-river 'flat-irons' built with collapsible funnel, mast and low bridge so as to be able to pass under the Thames bridges. An order for three 19,000 dwt colliers was placed with British Shipbuilders' Govan yard and all have now been delivered. Managed by Christian Salvesen, they are used principally to supply the two major coal-users, Tilbury 'B' and West Thurrock.

How these trends have affected the tonnage of coal handled in the Thames is best seen in the annual figures. From a total of 13.6 million in 1964, it had fallen to 6.43 million in 1971 and to 3.6 million by 1974. The figure increased slightly to 4.6 million in 1983, so that the trade seems to have settled down to between 3 and 4 million tonnes per annum.

A number of other berths on the Thames is also restricted to certain commodities. In 1984 there was a good traffic in sea-dredged

aggregates, totalling 5.4 million tonnes — the best figure for some years — which go to a number of wharves. Van den Bergh and Jurgens at Purfleet take in oils and fats for the production of *Flora*, *Spry* and *Stork* among others. Blue Circle has its own wharf near Northfleet for the handling of bulk cement, while next door is Bowater-Scott's facility for importation of its own pulp, timber and paper. A £2 million modernisation scheme was completed here in 1979. Apart from the refineries, oil products are also handled at tank farms. Esso has a large installation at Purfleet, while the independent oil storage depots at Canvey Island and Dagenham are owned by London and Coastal oil wharves. This company started operations in 1936, and now receives by sea some 500,000 tonnes per annum, most of which is distributed by road or pipeline.

Two other 'reserved' berths of particular interest are those owned by the Ford Motor Co and Tate & Lyle. The Ford Motor Co acquired the Dagenham site in 1925 because it was felt there was a need to be nearer Europe than at their Manchester plant, and Thames-side was an obvious choice. Production began in 1931, and the 'deep-water' facilities insisted upon by Henry Ford came into use. The plant and the

Left:
An aerial view of Ford's Dagenham plant in 1979 looking west. The tank farm near the top of the picture now belongs to London and Coastal, while sandwiched in between is the former Samuel Williams Dagenham Dock. *Ford Motor Co*

Below:
The Dagenham site and wharves being prepared for occupation by the Ford Motor Company in 1931. *Ford Motor Co*

wharf have been subject to a number of improvement schemes since then, and it is rare to pass the quay and not see a ship alongside, frequently a small container-ship carrying parts. The Silvertown factory and wharf now operated by Tate & Lyle originated in the period 1878-1881, when Henry Tate (later famous for his sugar lumps) and then Abram Lyle (equally well known for Golden Syrup) opened their businesses virtually next door to each other. The two concerns merged to form Tate & Lyle in 1921. The company no longer operates its own ships, but chartered vessels still bring in raw materials in quantity.

Yet another series of riverside berths can best be classified as 'general purpose' wharves, though some do concentrate on specific types of cargo. Of course, a great

Above:
The *Baltic Swift*, built in 1957, was one of a new generation of general cargo carriers operated by the United Baltic Company between London and the Baltic ports. Here she is arriving in the Pool in June 1962, actually passing *Baltrover* outwards. *Author*

Below:
An early photograph c1910 of Canadian Pacific's *Montezuma*, built in 1899, discharging cattle at Deptford. She would then convert cattle stalls to passenger berths for the outward passage to the St Lawrence. *Author's Collection*

Right:
Deptford Creek in 1946: the Channel Islands Company's *Nordic Queen* has arrived to discharge coal to rail wagons. *Ian Allan Library*

Below right:
Victoria Deep Wharf container terminal opened in 1973. The *Bell Renown* is alongside. Bell Lines have been using Victoria Deep since May 1976 when the Rotterdam service started. *Bell Lines*

Above:
A model of the Dartford International Freight Terminal as it should appear on completion.
Dartford Int Freight Terminal

Right:
Newsprint being discharged at Convoys Wharf in the 1950s. Deptford West Power Station is in the background, although now demolished. *Convoys*

number of these have closed down over the years, some of which were well known, including Instone's at Bow Creek in 1975, Samuel Williams at Dagenham and Palmers at Deptford in 1980, and Bruce's Wharf, Grays, in 1985, to name but a few.

It is worth having a closer look at some of the present-day river wharves. Starting at Tower Bridge and working downstream on the south bank, the first large concern is that of Convoys at Deptford, occupying part of the site of Henry VIII's Royal Dockyard. Founded in Southwark in 1920, Convoys moved to Deptford in 1926. In 1960 the company was taken over by the News of the World (later to become News International). Cargoes handled consist almost entirely of the importation of newsprint and other forest products coming primarily from the Baltic. The first ro-ro berth was opened in 1974, the second in 1981. Immediately below Greenwich is Lovell's Wharf, developed by C. Shaw Lovell and Sons, whose origins date from 1869. Steel and other metals, as well as some packaged timber, are predominant here. A little further round Blackwall Reach is Victoria Deep Wharf, part of the Scrutton's organisation. This is a specialist container berth, which started business for palletised general cargoes in 1967. The container terminal was commissioned in June 1973 by taking in and developing four adjacent wharves. Further

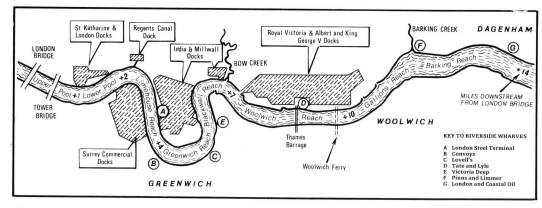

Above:
The River Thames (London Bridge to Dagenham) showing the location of enclosed docks and principal river wharves.

development and the installation of a second container crane were completed in 1981. The wharf is used by a number of lines, notably Bell and Ellerman for Portugal. Next downstream is Erith Deep Wharf, which, like its parent company Purfleet Deep Wharf on the north bank, specialises in paper and other forest products. Formerly Cory's coal wharf, it was taken over by Purfleet in 1967. A ro-ro berth was opened here in 1980.

The first all-new riverside development to be promoted for many years is situated near Dartford, close to the southern entrance of the Dartford-Purfleet tunnel. The £20 million ro-ro project was inaugurated in July 1985 as the Dartford International Freight Terminal. Owned equally by Blue Circle (who owns the land) and Municipal Mutual Insurance, the terminal on completion will cover some 60 acres, will have two berths (one on each side of a floating pontoon) and will be able to take ships of up to 11m draught at any state of the tide. The promoters hope that several ro-ro lines will use the new facilities. Tower Wharf at Northfleet, is also the UK berth for a number of shipping lines serving Rumania, Turkey, East Africa and the Middle East among a number of destinations. Baxter Fell bought the site in 1947 and developed it rapidly, at first for handling scrap metal. A second deep water

Below:
The River Thames (Dagenham to Gravesend) showing the location of enclosed docks and principal river wharves.

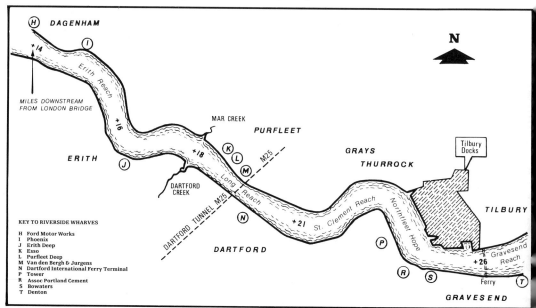

Above:
The Falkland Islands Company's *AES* discharging wool at Denton Wharf in May 1985. She makes four round voyages a year. *Author*

Left:
Looking south over Purfleet Deep Wharf, this view shows the extensive warehousing, railway connections and trailer parks. Finanglia's new *Finnmerchant*, 13,025dwt, is at the floating ro-ro terminal, while a conventional ship is being discharged at the railway berth. *Purfleet Deep Wharf*

Left:
A Mafi-trailer discharges packaged forest products from a Finnish ship at Purfleet in 1984. *Author*

Below:
A river view of the entrance to Bow Creek, showing the 'Guillotine' anti-flood barrier, and two ships working at Seabright's chemicals and fertiliser wharf in August 1985. *Author*

Right:
The steel terminal at Millwall operated by Freight Express-Seacon Ltd. The *Sea Merlan*, 1,575dwt, is discharging steel coil from the Rhine. *Author*

Below right:
Deanston Wharf was specially constructed in the early 1960s to handle tea in chests, delivered by lighter mostly from Ellerman and Clan ships. With the advent of containerisation it rapidly fell into disuse. *Author*

berth (the first was acquired with additional land in 1972) was started in 1979 and wider business was sought, particularly in the sphere of general cargo operations. A £3 million modernisation plan was completed in 1981. It is claimed to be the largest privately-owned general cargo terminal operating on the Thames. Last on the south bank is Denton Wharf, a bare one mile down river of Gravesend. Originally founded at Northfleet by

Hawkins Brothers in the early 1950s, the present site was taken over a few years later, and was quickly developed, a second deep water berth was completed in about 1977. The old isolation hospital was incorporated in the development, parts of which are in use as offices. All types of conventional cargoes are handled, as well as containers. The wharf is licensed for the acceptance of explosives. There are regular liner sailings to East

Germany, Turkey, Mediterranean and Middle East ports in addition to some further afield — including Central America and the Falkland Islands.

Moving back upstream, on the north bank, we find Purfleet Deep Wharf at Purfleet itself, sandwiched between Van den Bergh's and Esso. A berth here has been associated with timber since 1879, but it was not until 1963 that the first notable improvements were made

— two ships could now be accommodated. It was in that year when the Associated Newspapers Group acquired a small holding in the company, though three years later Purfleet Deep Wharf became a wholly-owned subsidiary. Like Erith Deep, Purfleet concentrates mainly on forest products, and in 1974 a new £3 million ferry terminal was opened, and in October 1984 Finanglia celebrated 10 years' continuous use for its Finnish run. The berth is

also used by Polanglia, a joint Polish Ocean-United Baltic operation, which celebrated its fifth anniversary of weekly ro-ro sailings to Gdynia in August 1985. Phoenix Wharf at Frog Island, Rainham, is the next upstream of any size. The company was originally founded in 1925 to handle timber imports through Surrey Commercial Docks, until they were bombed out in September 1940. Various berths were then used, until the company moved to Rainham in 1945. Here a wharf was constructed, using two 'Mulberry' pontoons and a Bailey bridge bought from the government. The first ship, the *Springtide*, berthed on 7 August 1948. Until Surrey Commercial closed, Phoenix took in only its own group timber, but after 1970 Russian timber began to be handled on a general basis for a wide range of receivers. As mentioned previously, Phoenix Wharf now handles bulk wine. Fertilisers, animal feeds and general cargoes also pass over the berths but timber is always predominant. The ro-ro berth was opened in 1978. Hidden up Barking Creek, and not seen from passing ships, is Pinns and Limmer Wharf. Started in about 1928 by Pinn and Wheeler Ltd, the berth first handled building materials, but after the war timber was of prime importance

until about 1969, when steel became predominant. Finally, in this brief survey of the larger river wharves, is the London Steel Terminal, situated on the Isle of Dogs half-way up Limehouse Reach. Opened in 1976 by Freight Express-Seacon Ltd, this specialises in importing steel. Equipment includes a 30-tonne travelling crane, and a canopy which extends 20m over the river, so that cargoes are protected from all but the worst weather.

Below:
On board ship, passing through the Thames Flood Barrier piers. The large building on the right, marked GLC, is the control centre. *Author*

Right:
The former GLC's new Thames fire-fleet, London Phoenix, was built by Fairey Marine, Cowes, and delivered early in 1985. She is capable of 11kt. *Author*

Below right:
Police river patrol boats at Wapping in 1985. There are 21 available for duty at all times. The smaller boats furthest from the camera are two of seven which were delivered during 1985. They are capable of 18kt, and are replacing a similar number of earlier boats built in the early 1960s, in the foreground. *Author*

Another aspect of river traffic apart from those already mentioned is lighterage. Once a common sight, a string of barges under tow for such places as Brentford with general cargo is now almost a thing of the past. Waste now comprises the most usual 'cargo', on its journey from up-river depots to the in-fill site at Rainham Marshes. The new Western Riverside Transfer Station, on land formerly occupied by Wandsworth Gas Works, was initiated by the GLC and opened in 1985. It can handle up to 4,000 tonnes of solid refuse per week. The new system involved the introduction of closed refuse containers which are then barged down-river, usually behind a Cory 'lighterage' tug.

Some plans which would have given rise to increased traffic include the Maplin project and the development of the Occidental refinery

Right:
**Watkins' steam tug *Gondia*,
built in 1927, seen off
Gravesend in March 1963.**
Author

Below:
**Oliver's Wharf seen from the
river in 1985. An example of late
Victorian Gothic architecture,
it has now been converted into
flats.** *Author*

at Canvey Island. Neither materialised. But the Thames anti-flood barrier did, and has proved its value since becoming operational in October 1982.

Only ship towage on the river remains to be mentioned here. The first 'organised' company to be established was W. Watkins in 1833, followed by T. W. Elliott in about 1860, Gaselee & Son in 1879 and Gamecock in 1880. After various changes of title, all the above, except Gaselee, centralised their fleet management in 1950 under a new company with the name Ship Towage (London). This was changed to London Tugs in 1969, when Gaselee joined in. Liverpool's Alexandra Towing Company took over London Tugs in 1975 and from then became the sole estuary and river towing company on the Thames, although it is true that certain smaller tugs from lighterage companies are used from time to time. It is interesting to note that the last tug built for Elliott, the *Avenger* constructed in 1962, was sold for further trading as recently as early 1986.

The Alexandra Towing Co (London) now maintains a fleet of about 12 tugs on the Thames, based on Gravesend, varying between 18 and 55 tonnes bollard pull.

Above:
Ellerman Wilson Line's *Electro*, built in 1937, loading at General Steam Navigation's Irongate Wharf for the Antwerp Steamship Co's service to Antwerp in June 1962. *Author*

Left:
It is difficult to believe that, by 1985, this was the same General Steam Navigation's Irongate Wharf, at left, with St Katharine's Wharf, centre. The Tower Hotel is now prominent, with the entrance to St Katharine Dock on the far right. *Author*

Below:
P&O used St Katharine's Pier for its continental services with the Jetfoil *Flying Princess*. The service started in June 1977 but was withdrawn in September 1980 due to lack of support. *Author*

Bibliography

The following is a list of selected books recommended for further reading:

General

The Port of London, R. D. Brown; (Terence Dalton, 1978)

Portrait of London River, Basil E. Cracknell; (Robert Hale, 1968)

Docklands History Survey, Preliminary Edition (Greater London Council, 1984)

Dockland; (GLC/North East London Polytechnic, 1986)

Liquid History, Arthur Bryant; (Port of London Authority, 1960)

Notes on the Port of London, (Port of London Authority, 1983)

London's Docks, John Pudney; (Thames and Hudson, 1975)

A Guide to the Thames, Adrian Prokter; (London Reference Books, 1983)

Specialised

Gas and Electricity Colliers, Chesterton and Fenton; (World Ship Society, 1984)

A Century of Sea Trading, L. C. Cornford; (John Black, 1924)

London's Waterways, Martyn Denney; (Batsford, 1977)

Royal River Highway, F. L. Dix; (David and Charles, 1985)

London, Tilbury and Southend Railway, George Dow; (Ian Allan)

Electricity Supply in the UK; (Electricity Council, 1982)

British Canals, Charles Hadfield; (David and Charles, 1979)

Semper Fidelis, H. E. Hancock; (General Steam Nav Co, 1949)

The History of Scruttons, A. E. Jeffrey; (Scruttons, 1971)

Thames Crossings, Geoffrey Phillips; (David and Charles, 1981)

Discovering London's Canals, Derek Pratt; (Shire Publications, 1977)

London's Lost Railways, Charles Klapper; (Routledge and Kegan Paul, 1976)

Thames Coast Pleasure Steamers, E. C. B. Thornton; (Stephenson, 1972)

Regional History of the Railways of Great Britain, Vol 3 Greater London, H. P. White; (David and Charles, 1971)

Journals and Periodicals

Port of London Authority: *Annual Reports, PLA Monthly, Port of London Magazine* (Quarterly), *The Port Newspaper*

Panorama: *The Journal of the Thurrock Local History Society*

Sea Breezes; Ships Illustrated; Ships Monthly; Syren and Shipping; Fairplay; Lloyd's List, Bygone Kent, etc, etc.

In addition, it should be noted that histories of shipping companies which are based in London — and of many which are not — give information on various aspects of activities in the port.